CW00705764

Yorkshiremen for All Seasons

Characters of the Three Ridings

by

Alex Marwood

Highgate Publications (Beverley) Ltd.
1992

i

British Library Cataloguing in Publication Data available

ISBN 0 948929 56 1

Published by Highgate Publications (Beverley) Ltd.
24 Wylies Road, Beverley. HU17 7AP.
Telephone (0482) 866826

Printed and Typeset in 10 on 11pt Garamond by
Colourspec, Unit 7, Tokenspire Business Park, Hull Road,
Woodmansey, Beverley. HU17 0TB.
Telephone (0482) 864264

ISBN 0 948929 56 1

PREFACE

Yorkshire was so huge a county that by the time William the Conqueror arrived it already had been split into three divisions, or Ridings, by the Saxons. When it was chopped into four new areas under the 1972 local government reorganisation there was a public outcry. The concept and names of the historic Ridings vanished at one stroke of the bureaucratic pen and we ended up with North Yorkshire, West Yorkshire, South Yorkshire and a place called North Humberside, linked with South Humberside, which in turn used to be part of Lincolnshire. Winifred Holtby, of course, fooled them all with her marvellous creation of 'South Riding', which some visitors spend a great deal of time searching for, usually ending up somewhere near Sheffield.

More than a century ago a Scottish couple of independent means, who had travelled widely and written a book about their rambles on the continent, turned their attention to this corner of England, which might just as well have been a foreign country to them. Their observations on the native inhabitants are as valid now as they were then:

'The people are most interesting; they are always kind and genial, full of a quaint racy humour and, in spite of their proverbial thrift, hospitable to strangers... [they] seem to have an utter contempt for Southerners, not only with respect for their powers of house-cleaning, but for their general capacity; indeed, it may be said of Yorkshire folk that they carry self-respect beyond a virtue. They seem to be a practical, sensible, but unimaginative race, and are therefore more likely to make money, and to keep it when made, than to understand or to do justice to qualities which they do not possess.'

Thomas and Katherine McQuoid were among the earliest recorded tourists in the county, which they travelled by train, by pony and trap and on foot. When they alighted at York they stayed at the 'new' Station Hotel. Their diary makes fascinating reading; they had the place almost to themselves - no coachloads of sunseekers bombing up to the Dales from the motorway - and each community was still virtually self-supporting, with its traditional craftsmen, home-grown food and entertainment. One or two tales in this book are distilled from their writings, some from much older sources, and others have been passed down to me by word of mouth.

We shall see the Yorkshireman as businessman, husband and lover, as holy and unholy, sportsman, eccentric, humorist; we shall see how he amused himself in days of yore, and how he took his revenge when crossed.

CHAPTER 1

PASTIME AND TRADITION

The Yorkshireman has always enjoyed a colourful spectacle, especially if it is part of an old-established tradition.

Pomp and Splendour

How did a martyred Armenian bishop come to be revered in the Heavy Woollen District of the West Riding? No one seems to know, and fewer today remember, but long ago it was the custom to hold a festival every seven years in honour of Bishop Blaise, who was the patron saint of woolcombers. In February, 1825, the occasion was held among unusual pomp and splendour.

Early in the morning, as the cock crowed, people set off from surrounding towns and villages to pour in a steady stream into Bradford. About 8 o'clock those taking part in the procession began to assemble in Westgate; and shortly before 10 o'clock they formed up under the supervision of Matthew Thompson Esquire. It made an impressive sight. The parade was headed by a herald bearing a flag. Then followed 24 woolstaplers on horseback, each horse caparisoned with a fleece. Thirty-eight worsted spinners and manufacturers were mounted on horseback, in white stuff waistcoats, each with a sliver of wool over his shoulder and a white stuff sash; the horses' necks were covered with nets made of thick yarn.

Had a modern television crew been there to cover the event it would have panned the length of this magnificent procession, and dwelt on aspects of the visual feast it provided. The parade included six merchants on horseback, with coloured sashes; three guards; masters' colours; three more guards; 56 apprentices and masters' sons on horseback, with ornamental caps, scarlet coats, white stuff waistcoats and blue pantaloons; Bradford and Keighley bands provided a rousing accompaniment as there came the macebearer, on foot; six guards, the King and Queen; six more guards; Jason; Princess Medea; guards again; the Bishop's chaplain; then Bishop Blaise himself. The person who took the role of the King was an old man named William Clough, from Darlington, who had taken the part on four previous occasions; that's over a 28-year stretch! John Smith acted as Jason. Another John Smith played Bishop Blaise; he had borne the pastoral crook on several other commemorations. His chaplain was James Beetham.

That was not the end of the panoply; the cavalcade was followed by a shepherd and shepherdess; shepherd swains; 160 woolsorters on horseback with ornamental caps and various coloured slivers of wool; 30 combmakers; charcoal burners; combers' colours; another band; 40 dyers with red cockades, blue aprons and crossed slivers of red and blue.

This glittering assortment stretched for half a mile through the streets and roads of Bradford, and did not disperse until 5 o'clock. Several beautiful flags were displayed along the route.

If the ornaments of the spinners and manufacturers looked neat and elegant, the apprentices and masters' sons stole the show with their caps decorated with ostrich feathers, flowers and knots in coloured yarn. The shepherd and shepherdess and their swains wore bright green. The woolsorters had a dashing appearance as their plumes were formed in the shape of a fleur-de-lis. The woolcombers themselves cut impressive figures in their old-fashioned, full-flowing wigs of combed wool.

It was a day to remember, but sadly it ushered in a disastrous year for the trade. For long the industry had proved extremely prosperous for the town and district. The workers, however, had become increasingly discontent with their wages. In June some 20,000 of them banded together under the leadership of a woolcomber named John Tester and, after trying vainly to get an advance on their already quite high wages, downed tools. Funds poured in from all over the country in support of the strikers, who for 23 weeks all but brought the trade in Bradford to a halt.

Then outside support began to falter and the strikers wavered. Matters were not helped when Tester absconded with part of the funds. On November 7 1825 the union was dissolved. But 1,200 of the woolcombers and weavers and 1,000 children could not find work, even at the old rates.

The poverty and heartbreak that this engendered was in stark contrast to the high spirits and flamboyant exhibition that had begun the year. Not surprisingly, it was feared it would be the last time the festival of Saint Blaise was held at Bradford, but happily the colourful festival was eventually revived, just over 25 years later.

Bishop Blaise, incidentally, suffered martyrdom in AD 316. For some odd reason he was considered good at curing sore throats. Perhaps because people were well advised to wear woollen scarfs round their necks!

A 'Different' Spectator Sport

Voting in a general election was not always the simple, private affair it is today. Until quite recent times there were all sorts of status qualifications for voters and, until the advent of the secret ballot, there was no hiding which way you voted. Electors could be persuaded in a variety of ways to make up their minds.

In the early 1800s, when electioneering became a spectator sport with a difference, two rival parliamentary candidates in Yorkshire were said to have spent £200,000 on election expenses. They were Lord Milton and the Hon Henry Lascelles (afterwards Earl of Harewood). During the 15-day-long poll in May 1807 when Hull-born William Wilberforce, the slave Emancipator, was a candidate, a keen struggle for the second seat developed between Lord Milton, a Whig, and Lascelles, a Tory, whose friends wound the entire county up into party spirit at prodigious expense. Every means of transport that money could buy was pressed into service to bring in the supporters; the roads were jammed with coaches, carriages, barouches, curricles, gigs, fly-waggons and even eight-horse military cars conveying voters from the remotest parts of the county to the hustings at York. It was hailed as one of the most celebrated contests in the history of electioneering.

On the first day Lascelles polled the greatest number of votes. On the second Lord Milton headed the poll. On the fifth day Lascelles was once again in the lead and held it until the 13th day, at the close of which the numbers stood at: Milton 10,313; Lascelles 10,254. Money was poured in to keeping the voters happy. Wilberforce, however, topped the poll, Lord Milton defeating Lascelles by a narrow majority. When news of his victory reached London the Whig families sported large orange favours on their horses' heads.

An interesting sidelight on the fervour that surrounded this event was when the Mayor of Leeds, Richard Bramley, unwisely seized a boy who had shouted 'Milton forever!' People quickly rescued the lad and so intimidated the Mayor that he called out a troop of horse soldiers and read the Riot Act to the populace.

On another memorable occasion, in 1812, Mr Robert Milnes of Monk Fryston Hall, Mr Henry Lascelles, Lord Pollington of Methley Hall and Mr Edward Hodgson of Stapleton Hall contested the two parliamentary seats for Pontefract. Lascelles spent an enormous sum of money on bribes for supporters and his regard for the welfare of electors was expressed in verse by his opponents:

'*Their votes secured they may in vain expect my further grace,*
For seven long years this paltry town shall never see my face.'

They also revealed that the slush money was coming from the profits of the family's sugar plantations in Barbados, which relied on slave labour from Africa. Lascelles, meanwhile, threatened his tenants with eviction if they failed to vote for him. Hodgson had an individual brand of corrupt practice: votes could be exchanged for rabbits through his agent at the Red Lion Inn.

Pontefract was the first constituency in the country to make use of the new Ballot Act in 1872. It was a by-election in which the Rt Hon Hugh Childers (Liberal) defeated Viscount Pollington (Conservative) by a majority of 80. A man called Jeremiah Briggs had patented an improved apparatus for voting by ballot, which involved the voter dropping numbered or lettered balls down a chute in a closed booth, precautions being taken that he did not drop in more than one. But the idea was rejected in favour of the ballot-form, which is still used today.

A newspaper of the time commented that, 'while the newfangled system of slipping your folded voting paper into a sealed box might be successful in securing its object, it unquestionably renders balloting day the very dreariest of all the glad new year'.

Within weeks, Pontefract's municipal elections came along and the town again made history by using the secret vote.

One of Pontefract's three original ballot-boxes was subsequently sent to the British Museum and another was for many years kept at the town's central library. Borrowers, not knowing the real purpose of its letter-box-type opening, would drop sweet papers and even odd coins into the slit.

The Great Football Plot

In olden days at Beverley, on the Sunday before the races began, lads from the surrounding villages challenged the youth of that town to a football match. There were as yet no FA rules and, indeed, the match would hardly be recognisable nowadays as football. It bore more of a resemblance to the Eton wall game. For the aim was to get the ball from the grandstand at the racecourse down into the town and the goal was in North Bar Street, opposite St Mary's Church.

At one such event, in the Georgian period, the battle was unusually hard and the villagers had fought the Beverley lads every inch of the way into the town. Bob Spence, the butcher, saved their honour by kicking the ball from the corner of the Rose and Crown right over the North Bar. It was a kick that lived on many years afterwards as veterans boasted about it over their pipes and ale on an evening.

The rush through the North Bar had been terrific. Sammy Hall, the Mayor, happened to be leaving the nearby church with his escort of officers, a bit of bad timing you might say, for they were overthrown and trampled on the ground. Vowing vengeance, Sammy struggled to his feet and dusted himself off. Secretly though he had laid his plans to have the event suppressed, they leaked out and plot and counter-plot were laid as the day for the traditional contest came round again. It was a sunny morning with daisies bedecking the Westwood. People began to drift in from the villages, mingling with the townspeople, who had only one topic of conversation that day: the great football match.

The rumours of the Mayor's impending action against the footballing tradition were being whispered about, too, and some of the participants hung nervously around St Mary's Church, where the Mayor was at morning service. As His Worship emerged he greeted them with a sinister smile, which boded ill for success of the sports. However, it quickly went out of people's minds as they wended their way up to the Westwood and soon the grandstand was filled with the usual company of spectators, tradesmen and the better class of inhabitants of the town and their wives and friends.

As soon as the clock on St Mary's struck three, the players took sides and prepared for action. No one is sure how many were thus engaged, or what system of attack and defence they deployed. But there was a focal point: the instant when Bill Hartley, landlord of the Globe Inn, threw the ball into the air. The two sides engaged and from the mêlée the ball emerged, under the control of the Beverley contingent, who dribbled, passed and headed it towards the town. At one point it rolled towards a hedge... right where lay George Ruddock, the town's bellman. Concealed in plain clothes, he sprang to his feet, grabbed the ball and made for the hedge, on the other side of which he had a horse waiting for him, held by a constable.

George reached the hedge but found to his dismay that it was too high at that point for him to stride over, so he set about clambering across it. Just as he reached the top, one of the footballers, Bob Pratt, who was something of a boxer, caught him by the heel and held on until his mates came running up. Then they dragged poor George Ruddock along the top of the hedge, face down, for several yards. It is to be remembered that the hedge was stout and thorny and this merciless treatment all but disembowelled the bellman.

However, George no longer had possession of the ball. At the instant he was seized, he had tossed it to Robert Kemp, one of the town's sergeants. Running to intercept it, this worthy had slipped and fallen on his knees. Another player, John Hardman, had by now crossed the hedge, and hurled a chunk of stone at the sergeant, which bounced off his hatless head, leaving him senseless and out of the game. The footballers recovered the ball and the other constables, waiting to play their part in the diversion, retreated.

The game was resumed without further interruption and the Beverley men once more came out on top. So far as they were concerned, too, the Mayor was beaten. But the urge for revenge still burnt inside him and when the next contest came round again he had made further secret plans. As the great assembly turned up at the Westwood that May Sunday in 1825, it was felt to be perhaps an omen that the grass was no longer its emerald green; a premature hot, dry spell had scorched it brown. At three o'clock the ball was thrown up and the players surged forward. The ball was being moved towards Walkington but the Beverley lads threw in an extra effort and turned it back towards the town.

Then a roar went up from the stands. It was not the massed acclamation familiar to football fans the world over, but a warning: 'Look out, the soldiers are coming!' All eyes turned. They saw the Mayor, riding a grey horse, at the head of some 40 militia. Play halted as the force approached them. The Mayor read the Riot Act, his voice at times drowned by rowdy protests and offensive remarks. As if to show their contempt, the players turned away and resumed their game. The order was given to the militia, who fixed bayonets and charged the players, who broke up before them. Then the soldiers wheeled round and charged again, breaking the players up into smaller groups. Before long, the game was abandoned - and it proved to be the last of its kind although, like Bob Spence's famous kick, it would be the talk of the town for long to come; for, unhappily, a number of the footballers were sentenced to hard labour for their part in the fray.

A Mighty Blast

One of Yorkshire's oldest traditions is that of blowing the horn in Ripon Market Place each evening at nine o'clock. It may be said that this practice, now a great focal point for tourists to the area, has gone on from time immemorial. Originally, it marked the start of a period of protection that inhabitants enjoyed from loss through robbery, which lasted until sunrise. For this, they paid fourpence a year, but if they had a back door onto another street, from which they might risk double danger, then they paid eightpence. The corporation undertook to make good any loss suffered during this period.

Although the tax has long been discontinued and other more modern forms of insurance adopted, the horn is still blown by the Wakeman, as the official is called. Among the mightiest horn-blowers was one Benjamin Simmonds, who died in April 1846, after holding office for 30 years. His epitaph was:

'But now no more they'll hear his blast,
For Benjamin has blown his last. '

CHAPTER 2

BUSINESS AND INDUSTRY

Yorkshiremen are nothing if not industrious. They are renowned for their hard-working qualities as well as their sound business heads. They are also resourceful, inventive and far-seeing, with strong traits of honesty, generosity and thrift, as these examples show.

Bringing in Steam Power

The town of Ossett, near Wakefield, had a centuries-old tradition of making broad woollen cloth. Most folk who lived there were engaged in the business of weaving; and in those days business meant busy-ness. Up to just over a hundred years ago they were expected to toil at their looms for 15 hours every day of the week for eightpence (old money, that is). A horn was blown at five in the morning to signal their start and again at eight at night, knocking-off time. The products of their labours were taken to Leeds by the clothiers. They had to stand in Briggate in all weathers waiting to sell their goods.

About the year 1736 Richard Wilson, of Ossett, made two pieces of broad cloth. He carried it to Leeds on his head. The merchant who bought it wanted another piece to go with it, so Richard Wilson walked back to Ossett, picked it up and took it back to Leeds, all in the same day. It was a 40-mile trip all told.

Between that relatively minor happening and the next only a few decades elapsed - but an industrial revolution had been born.

No one is certain which of the partners in the Bradford woollen firm of Rambotham, Swaine and Murgatroyd successfully paved the way for the introduction of steam-power into the industry. It took a brave man to do what he did, and one wonders what would have happened had he not done so. It was in 1798 that the firm built the first mill to be worked by steam, in the 'Holme'. The engine which was to provide the motive force for the mill was of 15 horsepower, a respectable complement for the day. Fears about the use of steam power had turned the general population of the area against the idea of factories. So when a man began conveying stones for building the mill, a large body of local people gathered in his way, some of them seizing the horse's head to prevent further passage.

Fortunately, one of the partners in the firm was on hand. We don't know which one it was, but he was a man of some pugilistic prowess, and without ado he took off his coat and with his bare fists cleared a way through the crowd. This gave second thoughts to the demonstrators, many of whom realised the delicacy of their position under the law. They soon gave way and allowed the horse and cart to proceed. Without this unsung act of heroism the establishment of the steam-powered mills which raised Bradford to its formidable eminence might have been delayed.

Sadly, the coming of machinery into industries like weaving and, in the Midlands, lacemaking, combined with the commercial depression during the latter years of the Napoleonic War to produce outbreaks of unrest, the likes of which had not been seen since the Civil War. Large numbers of workers were thrown out of jobs and, to make matters worse, the prices of ordinary commodities rose. In Nottingham the stocking weavers banded together under the leadership of a self-styled general, Ned Lud, and smashed thousands of the newly-invented stocking frames. Not long afterwards, bodies of armed men appeared in Yorkshire. They broke into mills at Rawdon, near Leeds, and destroyed machinery. The same happened at Wakefield, the mob numbering about 300. In May 1812 the Sheffield militia's store-house was raided and arms and ammunition carried off. Two nights later a veritable miniature army descended on Mr William Cartwright's mill at Rawfolds, Liversedge. Mr Cartwright, helped by four of his own men and five soldiers, greeted the attackers with a volley of musketry. But the assailants, who were armed with blunderbusses, pistols, hatchets and muskets, broke down some doors and forced their way into the mill. Thanks to the gallant defence of the mill-owner and his tiny force, the mob withdrew, nursing several wounded.

Their action caused a great stir of excitement and a public subscription fund was launched, which raised £3,000. This sum was given to Mr Cartwright and his family.

So far the Luddites had intended only to destroy the hated machinery. Now their aim included shooting the factory masters as well. Mr William Horsfall, a Marsden manufacturer of note, was marked out for assassination. George Mellor, William Thorpe, Thomas Smith and Benjamin Walker ambushed Mr Horsfall as he returned from market at Huddersfield. He fell under a fusillade of shots and died a few days later. Mr Cartwright was also shot at on the road and attempts were made to 'eliminate' General Campbell, who commanded troops at Leeds. After a rampage through the industrial West Riding which left a trail of destruction on a massive scale, the Yorkshire Luddites were brought to book. Wholesale executions and transportations followed. One cannot help feeling that the original motivation behind their actions degenerated into an excuse for general vandalism and robbery, and that, had not the authorities acted as swiftly as they did to contain it, the county might have sunk into an era of brigandry as dark as that of earlier centuries.

Gifts To The World

Yorkshire has been the birthplace of many a sound idea, with the creator not content to sit around and mull it over. Translated into action, these flashes of insight have provided the world with some useful amenities.

How many people, for instance, know that a Yorkshire firm pioneered the use of fibreglass? In 1837 Richard Baker and Son, of Ossett Street Side, Dewsbury, so improved the manufacture of glass that they could make a cloth or fabric of the finest texture. From some of this finely-textured, pliable material they made some splendid ladies' head-dresses and ornaments. The following January the manufacturers presented an elegant glass apron to Queen Victoria, which looked like and felt like silk!

Without the inventiveness of John Harrison, of Pontefract, we should never have sailed the far seas and plotted accurately the latitude and longitude of the many countries we came to call our own. It was, he decided, all very well making a clock which could keep good time on someone's mantelpiece - but what about one that could cope with extremes of temperature and the constantly rolling motion of a ship? For in order to determine precisely one's position at sea it was necessary to know Greenwich Meantime to within ONE second. A carpenter's son, Harrison invented a pendulum composed of different metals, which suffered neither shrinkage nor expansion, thus maintaining an even swing. He also designed a clock which remained undisturbed by the motion of a ship. From his various brilliant ideas he put together a chronometer, a kind of super-accurate clock that gave navigators just what they wanted. He also earned a prize of £20,000, a huge sum in the 18th century, from the Royal Society. Not bad for a humble carpenter's lad!

Not so happy with the outcome of his own researches was a Leeds clockmaker named John Galloway. He spent most of his life in a fruitless quest for the secret of perpetual motion.

The development of the straw hat trade in this country owes much to the creation of a Beeston woman, Mrs Isabel Denton. Necessity was truly the mother of invention, for she had a husband who drank and gambled away every penny that came into the family purse during the reign of Charles I. Under circumstances that have not come down to us, she devised a simple method of making headgear in many shapes and styles using the plentiful supply of straw. She was thus able to support her family in comfort and respectability despite her husband's profligate excesses. During her lifetime, one Leeds firm is said to have sold £7,000 worth of straw bonnets in a year.

But ask around who invented the water closet, the fountain pen, and the hydraulic press; and took out patents for improved fire engines, carriage brakes and suspension, and printing machines. If you add to this impressive list the name of a famous lock, and the name may click, but not with many: Joseph Bramah. For sheer all-round genius this son of a Silkstone farmer takes some beating. It was misfortune that put him on the road to fame, for, while taking part in games at the annual Bolton-on-Dearne feast, he hurt his leg, which left him lame for life. While convalescing, he decided to make his pastime of wood-carving his trade.

After his apprenticeship, however, the county lost him to the attractions of London, where he was to set up a factory and develop his many ideas, particularly the harnessing of hydraulic power, which became a corner-stone of today's engineering technology.

Even the man at the workbench showed plenty of ingenuity. A smith who worked at Lofthouse once came up with a scheme for operating a hammer with his foot, while he used his left hand to hold the iron and the right to strike with the second hammer. This expedient saved him the expense of having to employ a labourer.

Perhaps the county's two most hapless 'inventors' were James Berkenhout, descended from a Dutch merchant, and Thomas Clarke, both of Halton, near Leeds. They went around proudly showing everyone samples of linen and cotton cloth dyed in the most gorgeous scarlet, crimson and other hues. The Government granted them £5,000 if they would make known their secret process, but they failed to reproduce colours of such quality again. It is probable that their samples had been produced by accident rather than by design, and there was a precedent for this. Not many years before, at Barnard Castle, a dyer's boiling kettles had been suddenly flooded by the Tees. Something in the water produced such a beautiful shade in the cloth then being processed that it sold at greatly improved prices. Orders poured in, but the poor dyer was never able again to produce the same striking effect.

As a matter of interest, a descendant of Mr Clarke occupied the White Bridge Mill at Halton until 1857, where he manufactured bunting for ships' colours. There, the first power loom in England was at work long before this type of machinery became known to the general public.

Crowds gathered on the banks of the Aire at Leeds on January 23 1720 to watch a Mr Robertson perform what he had promised would be an unparalleled spectacle. From a handkerchief he produced a small packet which he unfolded into the shape of a pliable boat made of thinnest leather. This he inflated with a pair of bellows and proceeded to cross the river, to the applause of 5,000 spectators. Unfortunately, it has to be admitted that Mr Robertson was born in France, of Scottish parents. But at least he tried out his invention in Yorkshire!

Trouble Over A Goat

Malton was always the busiest of places on Market Day. Farmers poured in from Ryedale and the Wolds with their horsedrawn wagons, and drovers packed the narrow streets with their flocks of sheep and beasts in twos and threes, so that the whole town throbbed with life. The pubs did a roaring trade, for bargaining was thirsty work, and many a deal was sealed over lunch and a tankard of ale.

A great deal of business was also concluded in the market area itself, with the slapping together of right hands a frequent accompaniment to the tide of lowing, crying, squealing, braying, bleating, calling, shouting and barking that rose and fell incessantly.

Among all this hubbub two farmers renewed old acquaintance. One was leading a splendid goat on a short tether.

'Eh, now,' remarked his companion. 'That's a fine goat you have there.'

The owner agreed that it was, knowing full well that the other man had had his eye on the animal since they met, and had been weighing it up discreetly.

The upshot of it was that an offer was made, and declined, but, after some parleying, it was agreed that 'five pun' should change hands, and along with it, title to ownership of the goat: without any formal ceremony apart from the traditional handshake, for this was considered as good as a man's bond.

The original owner still had hold of the goat's halter with one hand, as the buyer was in no apparent hurry to take possession, and there was plenty of local news to swap. In his other hand he held the five-pound note, an impressive affair on white paper about the size of a handkerchief in those days. Time was passing so pleasantly that he had not thought to stow it away in his inside pocket.

After a while there was a lull in the men's conversation and they both at once became aware of a new sound among the background din, a sort of crunching.

'Oh heck!' cried the purchaser of the goat, his eyes bulging with horror at something going on behind the other man. At that same instant the man who had just sold the animal realised he was only holding a very small fragment of white paper. They both stared at the goat, which was looking very pleased with itself as its jaws champed rhythmically from side to side.

'Quick!' urged the seller. 'Get his mouth open!' One held the struggling animal while the other forced its jaws apart just in time to see a pulpy white mass disappearing down its throat.

'Stop him swallowing it!' yelled the other man. Immediately, a stranglehold went on the unfortunate goat, but, with a great heave, it managed to gulp down the note, although it could hardly breathe.

'Get some watter... and salt, or mustard... anything to make him bring it up!' shouted the seller. An urchin who was watching the proceedings with fascination gladly accepted a penny to run to the nearest hotel and get these items and was quickly back with them, in a borrowed bucket. The goat struggled in vain as the two men again forced its mouth open and dosed it with the horrible mixture. It shook its head, eyes rolling, and gasped, but resolutely its stomach, accustomed to taking in stronger substances than that, refused to eject its contents.

The farmer who had sold the goat was panicking now. 'Only one thing for it,' he decided, pulling out a large clasp knife and preparing to open the blade. 'I want my five pun' back!'

'And I want my goat alive!' cried his companion, laying a restraining hand on the other's arm.

A small crowd had gathered to watch the dispute, in which the poor goat was now being tugged backwards and forwards between the two men. There was some merriment among the spectators; others were placing wagers on the outcome. Unhappily, dear reader, at this point the original account whence this little drama came had been torn off, and the outcome of the dilemma must be left to your own imagination. Were there in the end two losers? Did they go to law over the issue? Both unlikely solutions, for the Yorkshireman, especially of the rustic variety, hates to lose out all round, though he will gladly avail himself of 'summat for nowt'.

What's your verdict, then? My guess is that they agreed to auction the goat and split the proceeds between them.

The Test Of Temptation

Honesty is a strong Yorkshire characteristic; but beware taking undue advantage of it. Young Benjamin Swales was apprenticed to a small shopkeeper at Richmond at the turn of the last century. The shopkeeper was a Scotsman by the name of Rab Mc-Something-or-Other; at any rate, Benjamin found it difficult to pronounce and was forever getting into trouble for referring to his employer in these terms within customers' hearing. As this is supposed to be a book about Yorkshireman, we'll just refer to the Scotsman as Rab.

Whether it was because of this, or on account of his celebrated national instinct for thrift, Rab determined to put his youthful helper's honesty to the acid test. Part of Benjamin's daily duties included keeping the bare wooden floor of the shop swept clean and polished; especially at the close of the day's trade, which was usually well into the evening. Rab put into action a devious ploy which he had learnt from his grandfather, who had been a tailor in Paisley: while Benjamin was engaged in work in the back part of the shop, and no customers were about, he carefully concealed a halfpenny among some rubbish that had accumulated at the back of the counter.

Benjamin duly handed the coin to the shopkeeper after he had finished his chores, and Rab took this both as a sign of diligence in cleaning out all the corners of the premises as well as of honesty. But just how far could the lad be tempted, he mused? Next day, Rab hid a penny among some shavings in another corner. Again, the coin was returned.

After waiting for a few days, Rab wedged a silver shilling into a crack in the floorboards between two sacks of flour, where he would normally expect no one to look too closely. It was still there next morning, as a swift check revealed. Rab decided not to chastise the boy for neglecting to do his task thoroughly, but dropped a hint about the need to sweep well into all the corners of the shop at night. Sure enough, next day Benjamin came to his boss as he was about to lock up, holding the shilling out to him, without comment.

As a matter of fact, Benjamin's faultless honesty was becoming a challenge to Rab, who loved to find fault. He was also beginning to get a bit paranoid about his hard-earned money, imagining robbers were scheming to relieve him of it from its hiding place beneath his bed above the shop. It was with a real struggle that he brought himself to bait the trap he was hoping to spring on his apprentice with a whole sovereign, a gold coin that could bring untold wealth to a youngster in those days. After appropriating lesser sums, grown men had been known to run away and start new lives on the other side of the country. It was equivalent to a good day's profit for the shop, and Rab muttered Gaelic prayers to himself as he secreted it in a dusty corner under a ledge on the public side of the counter, where none of the customers would be likely to disturb it.

Came close of day and Benjamin had helped Rab to put up the heavy shutters, then swept and polished the floor. The shopkeeper stood expectantly by with his keys in his hand, waiting impatiently for Benjamin to turn in the missing sovereign. He had deliberately left the lad alone in the shop for a good ten minutes while he busied himself in the store room, in an agony of doubt over the wisdom of putting so large a sum at risk. Now he hovered anxiously about as Benjamin slipped on his tattered jacket and greasy cap and prepared to go to his lodgings.

Rab could stand the suspense no longer. He had sneaked a quick peek at the spot where he had laid the precious coin and he could see no sign of it. The woodwork was clean as new and shone with wax polish. There were no drifts of dust or dirt where it could be obscured.

'Have ye no' found anything today?' Rab inquired cautiously.

'Like what?' asked Benjamin.

'Weel, our customers can be a wee bit careless with their purses, and ye've been turning up a pretty penny or two of late. For which,' he added, 'we are very thankful to ye.'

Benjamin turned at the door to say goodnight, and Rab hurriedly put in: 'And what did ye do with the rubbish ye swept up tonight, then?' He had even ferreted around in the thick brown paper sugar bag that served as wastebasket, the contents usually helping to keep his hearth blazing.

'Ah,' replied Benjamin, as if the matter was of such small importance that it had already gone out of his mind. 'There wasn't much, so I threw it outside.'

'Outside?' declared Rab.

'In the gutter. It'll soon wash away.'

You have to understand that gutters were not always as we know them today. They were more like open sewers, awash with a horrid blend of refuse, human and animal, mixed with mud, straw, watered by the ever-present horse and dog, and generally of a not very savoury nature. On that evening it had not rained, and the rubbish that choked the long narrow gulley set at the pavement's edge was undisturbed. Undisturbed, that is, until the Scotsman rushed past young Benjamin and threw himself on his hands and knees and began scrabbling in the filth with his bare hands.

Scarcely able to contain himself, Benjamin tiptoed behind the frantic figure and made his way home; meanwhile a group of urchins had gathered round the curious spectacle of Rab the Scotsman engaged in an incomprehensible ritual. Happily to say, he found the sovereign, after a mere ten minutes' grovelling with his bare hands; he almost missed it, for it was embedded in a piece of singularly pungent horse-manure.

And that was the end of his honesty tests.

Surprise In The Post

The number of letters posted in Leeds doubled on January 10 1840, the day when uniform penny postage came into operation. Within a few weeks the number had increased fivefold. The new postage brought letter-writing within reach of almost everyone, and replaced a system which limited this form of communication to those with plenty of ready cash. Hitherto, it had been the recipient of the letter who paid for it! This meant that for an Irish labourer in London to send a letter to his mother in Ireland she would be charged more than one-fifth of her son's weekly wages. A genius called Rowland Hill - brother of an MP for Hull - worked out that, although it cost only a trifling fraction of a penny to send a letter from to Edinburgh, a charge of one shilling and fourpence was made. Therefore he campaigned for the introduction of a uniform penny postage rate, to which, strangely enough, the Post Office was violently opposed, being an inefficient business run on the lines of a secret service and regarded by the government as sacrosanct. Its introduction was widely denounced, the then Postmaster-General describing it as 'the wildest scheme he had ever heard of'.

Not many years before Rowland Hill brought about this momentous advance, a poor weaver named David Lindsey, who lived in Manchester, was sitting in his humble cottage, making the most of his meagre breakfast of bread without butter and coffee without sugar, when the postman knocked on his door. (I know Manchester is not in Yorkshire and this is a book about Yorkshire, but there is a point to including this story here, as you will see!) A postman was a rare enough person to see about in those days, and even as he arrived at the weaver's home the neighbourhood was agog to know what was going on.

'That'll be four shillings and ninepence!' demanded the postman, clutching a missive on heavy quality paper, folded on itself to make an envelope, and sealed with red wax. The address was neatly written in a flowing hand, but, of course, David could not read it, being illiterate. He was overcome with excitement and his wife and three children hurried to the door to see what was going on.

'Who can it be from?' asked the poor weaver.

'Not allowed to tell you that, young sir,' replied the postman, hugging the letter close to his chest as if afraid it might be snatched from him.

'Oh dear, dear,' said the weaver, wringing his workworn hands. 'Nobody would want to send a letter to me... and I could never afford to pay for receiving one. Surely there has been some mistake?'

The postman glanced officiously at the letter and confirmed that it was indeed at its destination. By now he was impatient to be on his way, for he had letters to deliver to grander folk on the other side of town who he knew would reward him with a small tip, or even an invitation to share cake and tea with the butler, especially if the news he brought was good news.

The weaver and his wife rummaged through their pitifully few belongings and failed to come up with more than a few pence in cash set aside for their next meal. And David knew that the equipment he worked with had been bought secondhand for less than nine shillings and if he could find a buyer at such short notice would fetch only three or four shillings - but then he would be without a means of earning his living, so what would be the point, when there could not possibly be anything in this letter to interest him?.

'Well, then,' declared the postman, 'it'll have to go back to the office.' And he made ready to turn about, tucking the letter in his leather satchel.

'Hang on a minute!' came a voice, and a bluff, stocky man pushed through the small crowd that had gathered. 'What's this is all about? Is our David in trouble?' It was a close-knit community and the use of 'our' reflected the spirit that bound it together. David recognised the man as a small shopkeeper to whom he had on occasion owed 'tick' to feed his family, but to whom he had never failed to make good his credit.

The postman brusquely explained the situation. The man's eyes lit up. 'Ah've a feeling there could be summat in this letter.' (Now you see why this story is included. Enough said.) 'Four and nine, you said? Here's five bob. Buy yourself a drink with the change!'

The postman scowled, like something cheated of its prey, and grudgingly handed over the letter, which David took in trembling hands.

'It's nobbut a loan, sitha,' said his benefactor. 'Oppen it, quick like, I just know there's summat important inside.'

David fumbled at the seal, never having had a letter to open before. Then he handed it mutely to the man, who took it and deftly opened it out, tracing the words with a stubby forefinger as he read it silently to himself. He looked up at David. 'Let's go inside, shall we? I think this could interest thee.'

The spectators, who had pressed close to goggle at the letter - not one of them could have read it, anyhow - fell back as the two men went inside and closed the door. The weaver's wife stood by his side, anxiety written all over her face.

'Got an uncle in Scotland, haven't you?' quizzed the man. The weaver couldn't think of one. 'Well, you have. Colonel Lindsey, elder brother of your late father. He's died.'

The weaver shrugged his shoulders. He'd gone into debt to the local shopkeeper for five whole shillings just to learn that a man he'd never heard of had died! His wife clapped a trembling hand to her mouth in horror.

'Seems he had a bit of land... in Cupar, Fife. Never heard of the place myself...'

'What about the bit of land?' exclaimed the weaver, picking up a sense of excitement as the reader deliberately hung back on the message savouring the words.

'Well, lad, to cut it short and to the point...'

'Yes?'

'You've come into his estate of, oh, £300,000, give or take a bob or two, as he has no one else to leave his fortune to. And his solicitors, who have gone to immense trouble and expense to trace you, his only surviving relative, have been thoughtful enough to enclose the sum of one £150 to defray the expenses of your journey up there with your family to take up residence at your country seat.'

At this point we take our leave of this touching tableau: David Lindsey, the poor weaver, stunned beyond belief; his wife, nearly fainting from shock, the children screaming and shouting, folk outside banging on the door asking if they were all right, and faces crammed against the single grimy window. And the shopkeeper shaking David's hand like a water-pump, his face wreathed in congratulatory smiles.

Somewhere in Scotland today there are two well-to-do families, one descended from a destitute Manchester weaver, the other from a former Yorkshire exile to Lancashire who offered to show him the way there and see he took good care of his investments.

Public Paid Ransom

The Yorkshireman's readiness to dip his hand in his pocket for a good cause is well illustrated by this account of how a public appeal freed a kidnap victim some 300 years ago. A Leeds alderman named Foxcroft had put his son out as an apprentice to Mr Robert Newport, captain and owner of the *Adriatic*. While on a voyage, the young apprentice became ship's purser and when the ship's master unfortunately died he had to take over most of the running of the vessel.

When Turkish pirates boarded the ship near Algiers, they mistook the capable young Yorkshireman for the captain himself, and obstinately refused to believe that he was merely an apprentice. Without further ado, they clapped him in irons and carried him off to Algiers, where they sold him to middlemen in the kidnapping business for 700 dollars. It was decided he should be ransomed for the sum of £350 sterling, and under some duress he wrote a letter home to his family in Leeds describing his predicament and the conditions for his release from it.

His father, though a man of some substance, did not have this sort of ready, and appealed to the local court to help him with his son's redemption. The magistrates ordered that a house-to-house collection be made in the borough, with the aim of freeing 'a Christian soul from the hands of those barbarous infidels'. The court also ordered that a letter be written to Hull, asking for charitable contributions. Eventually, through widespread public donations, the young man was restored to his native county, none the worse for his adventures.

Rush For Baptism

Just because he is generous at heart does not mean the Yorkshireman is not careful with his money. If he could spend a shilling now to save two later, he always would. When an Act that came into force on July 1 1837 for the registration of all births, marriages and deaths, hundreds of Yorkshire families believed - mistakenly - that it would increase baptismal fees. Now, many folk had delayed having their children baptised, probably balking at the cost; but now there was a great rush to get any done that had missed. At Huddersfield, 86 were baptised in one day; at Bradford, anxious parents crammed the churches to bring a total of 398 children to the font; this figure at Leeds for the same period topped 400.

CHAPTER 3

AFFAIRS OF THE HEART

Although outstandingly practical in most matters, the Yorkshireman possesses a romantic streak which occasionally allows his heart to run away with his head. Since his temperament, however, is not that of the hot-blooded Latin, he has not occasioned any great idylls on the lines of Romeo and Juliet. Yet the county has provided one or two touching little romantic interludes...

Lady Of The Manor

The terraces and woods of Duncombe Park overhang the lovely Rye as it wends its way past Helmsley; and in this beautiful setting this story is said to have unfolded. But is it a great love story or a tale of well-concealed ambition?

It is said that many years ago the lord of the manor, an ancestor of the Fevershams - who in recent times returned to their traditional home after it had served for many years as a girls' school - was riding home when he noticed a girl in a sun bonnet swinging to and fro on the gate to the park. He reined up his horse and heard that she was singing softly to herself:

> *'It may so happen, it may so fall*
> *That Ah may be lady o' Duncombe Hall.'*

Then she turned to look at the young squire, and he found himself gazing into the prettiest face he had ever seen. And he fell headlong in love with this wonderfully lovely girl. Whether she happened to be there by chance, singing what was perhaps a children's playground song of the time, or whether she had secretly taken a fancy to his lordship, 'set her cap' at him as they say in Yorkshire, and had carefully contrived the encounter, no one will ever know. But the outcome was that he persuaded her parents to send her to a quality school for some years at his own expense (she was only 14 years old when they met).

When she returned from school she was well educated and groomed, had acquired social graces from the daughters of the gentility she had rubbed shoulders with, and was even more beautiful than the squire remembered. So he proposed to her, and without further delay they were married, and the young lady became mistress of Duncombe.

Unfortunately, her name has not come down to us, but it is presumed that somewhere in the family archives it can be found.

A Bridge Of Sighs

There lies a tale of sheer determination behind the Beggar's Bridge, which spans the River Esk in one soaring arch not far from Whitby. It was supposedly built by an Egton man who loved a lass from Glaisdale - on the other side of the river. He was so poor that he couldn't afford to cross by ferry, so he used to ford the water, often wading up to his thighs in order to spend an hour or two with his beloved. ··

There came the time when he joined a Whitby ship financed by merchants to travel to far-off seas in search of trade; for there he saw his chance to make something out of his life. On what was to be his last night on Yorkshire soil for several years he went to bid his lover farewell. But the rains had been heavy and the Esk was swollen and turbulent. Twice he tried swimming across but was swept back to his own side. Finally, he sighed and gave up. He climbed back up the hillside from which, in the distance, he could see the glimmering light of the cottage where he longed to be wrapped in her arms. He vowed there and then that if he ever returned with a fortune he would build a bridge across the water at that very point. Which he did!

The amorous bridge builder was Thomas Ferries, famous in the history of Hull as one of it's greatest benefactors - though his gifts did not include a bridge across the Humber.

Passion and Intrigue

But it was a story of more deeply-running passion and intrigue from nearby Whitby that inspired Mrs Gaskell to write *Sylvia's Lovers* and which reflects without too much sentimentality the harsh existence of a seafarer at that storm-lashed little port. For it was a fact that the hardy, weatherbeaten menfolk lived in constant fear of the pressgang, armed thugs with the government's authority to kidnap men to serve in the navy of the Empire-building 1700s. Not surprisingly, their womenfolk shared this dread.

There was no such shadow over Farmer Mossburn when he learned that his two pretty daughters had fallen in love with two brothers who went regularly on fishing trips to Greenland - just imagine the perils of such a voyage, at the mercy of wind and wave. Imagine, too, the joy with which they returned home safely and set off once more to visit their sweethearts. Not far out of town they met a young woman called Polly, with whom they paused to chat. Suddenly, she said something to the youngest of the lads, Bill that quite shook him: that she had awfully missed seeing him, and that she desired more of his company.

'Nay, lass,' he replied, 'Ah cannot gan wi' you. Ah've other fish to fry.' It was true that they had shared a joke now and then in times past, but there was never anything serious between them.

Polly was a tall, strongly-built girl with rough reddish hair and a freckled face. She fixed her pale blue eyes intensely on the young sailor.

'Ista thinking on Hester Mossburn?' she asked scornfully. 'She's not for you, Bill.'

Bill's brother Peter broke this awkward conversation, then Polly ran off, crying, 'Curse her! Curse the pair of 'em!' until her voice died on the moortop wind.

The incident was soon forgotten as with time-honoured courtesy the brothers made known their feelings about the two girls to their father, and, after much debate far into the night, a date was fixed for a double wedding. Hester's sister Dorothy went outside with Peter for a protracted farewell kiss and a cuddle. Her mother, tut-tutting, was just about to go out to fetch her in when she heard her scream.

'T'pressgang, they've gotten Peter!'

Bill and the girls' father dashed outside but were powerless against a squad of muscular toughs; they laid Farmer Mossburn out with a bludgeon, and dragged Bill into a boat to lie bound and gagged beside his brother. The girls shrieked and wept helplessly as the boat was rowed off into the mist.

Months went by and occasional reports arrived of great sea-fights in which the English had been glorious victors. But to the two sisters this only meant more chance that their beloved ones had been killed. They donned mourning clothes, their pale, drawn faces stirring glances of sympathy from the Whitby folk. From all, that is, except Polly, who took to mocking them openly. One day she boasted too much: if a lad broke faith with her, she knew how to punish him. 'Ye can ask Hester Mossburn,' she declared.

A shocked silence fell on the circle of fishermen and their lasses who had been a moment before swapping coarse jokes. One grizzled veteran of the seas grabbed her by the arm and fixed her with a steely glance, as if she were a fish on a hook. 'Ista false, Polly?' and without waiting for an answer, flung her from him. The man she collided with thrust her away as if she had the plague. Polly picked herself up and scowled. Her eyes went from stony face to stony face. Not a friend among them. Polly turned and fled. Her landlady turned her out of her home and no one would shelter her or give her a job. Finally, she took to the wild wastes of the moors, telling wayfarers that she was waiting for her lad. Shame and exposure to the elements took away her reason and she became known simply as 'Crazy Polly'.

This bitter story has a sweet ending, for the two brothers did eventually return to Whitby, although both had been seriously wounded on active service. Happy to relate, the two sisters were still waiting for them...

Wives For Sale

George Woodhead, of Leeds, married his wife Molly, a sweet young thing with soft brown hair and appealing blue eyes, in good faith. It wasn't long before he discovered that she had secretly married another man William Idle, a collier from Ouslewell Green, near Rothwell. How she managed to slip away for long enough to do this and, presumably, set up a second home, is a mystery; perhaps George was too busily engaged in his duties as servant to a farmer and butcher some distance away at Hemsworth, and she felt neglected.

However, George devised a particularly humiliating way to 'show her up' and rid himself of her at the same time. He sought out William Idle and told him: 'You've got her, you can keep her. But first meet me at Leeds butter and poultry market next Friday at noon. We'll settle this matter friendly, like.'

Then he took his faithless wife to the market with a length of rope round her neck, like a dog-lead, and publicly sold her to William Idle for the sum of five shillings.

But even in 1844 the rough and ready folk of that great woollen city still baulked at some things; and selling one's wife off like some common piece of livestock was a bit much. Someone reported the transaction to the authorities. Woodhead was brought before the magistrates, who bound him over to be of good behaviour for 12 months in a considerable sum of money. The wife was committed to York Castle charged with bigamy, for which she was imprisoned. And William Idle, lucky fellow, got off without any trouble at all, although he vowed never to trust another woman so long as he lived.

The public selling of one's wife had been something of a tradition in the West Riding. In 1808 a man is reported to have sold his wife at Leeds market for five guineas. The woman's mother was said to have been sold at the same place, while she was carrying her.

But the story of wife-selling that takes some beating is that of Mr Samuel Lumb, of Sowerby, who was 83 years of age in October 1827 when he married Mrs Rachel Heap, to whom he had already been espoused 25 years before. It came about like this. Her first husband had joined the army, and was given up for dead. So his 'widow' married Mr Lumb. In due course, the 'dead' soldier returned from the wars and found his wife living in a state of bliss with Mr Lumb, by whom she had had three children.

Mr Lumb and the soldier got together and thrashed the matter out. After some negotiation, Heap agreed to sell her, and Mr Lumb solemnly bought her, after she had been brought to Halifax market cross with a halter round her neck, as if she were a horse or a cow. Samuel Lumb then formally married his wife again. Just to complicate matters, she was given away at the altar by Lumb's grandson.

Ups and Downs Of Marriage

Marriage was, however, generally regarded as a serious matter. Just how much thought should go into it has never been officially laid down, but the union in June 1847 of Mr John Bright Esquire, a Member of Parliament, to Miss Leatham at Wakefield Friends' meeting house in George Street was certainly not a rushed affair. A large wedding party arrived there at half-past ten in the morning, and the whole company sat in total silence for three quarters of an hour, until Mr Bright rose, took Miss Leatham's hand, and recited an impromptu declaration of his intention of marrying, to which she replied in similar vein. Then prayers were said, and a certificate signed.

This was in sharp contrast with the offhand way a Wolds couple went to Acklam for their wedding. After the parson had read out the marriage vow the bridegroom just stood there without opening his mouth. The parson repeated the words. But instead of saying, 'I will', the bridegroom replied, 'I might as well, that's what I've come here for!'

Banns have long been read out in churches on three consecutive Sundays as a means of establishing if there is any impediment to a forthcoming marriage. No one seriously believes that there will be objections, but just such a scene occurred at Keighley church on a Sunday in March 1835. The curate was publishing the banns of marriage of a couple who both lived in the parish when the outspoken mother of one of the parties stood up and shouted, 'I forbid that!'

The wheels of love sometimes ran more smoothly. They certainly did in the case of a Leeds pair who eloped in 1846. At midnight Mr Joshua Burton, of Roundhay, put the proverbial ladder up to the window of his sweetheart, Miss Fanny Wilkinson, eldest daughter of John Wilkinson Esquire, of Gledhow, and dashed with her to a waiting post-chaise. They wasted no time speeding to Gretna Green, where they were married the next day at four o'clock in the afternoon.

Once hitched, things did not always go so well. A Major Bradley, of Leeds, advertised in October 1769 for news of his wife: she had left him for the 14th time.

Despite all these connubial ups and downs, a Yorkshireman knows a good thing when he sees it. In 1679 a Leeds merchant, Mr Thomas Potter, put up an epitaph in his parish church to the memory of his 'truly dear and vertuous wife Jane,' who had died at the tender age of 24. It read:

'This homely case a jewel doth contain,
But shew'd the world, and so laid up again;
With meek and chaste behaviour every grace
Inrich'd, which beautifies the mind and face.'
[NB: These spellings as in the original]

The Matrimonial Hoax

Nothing is sacred to the Yorkshireman when he is in jesting mood, as witness the great matrimonial hoax perpetrated at Leeds in September 1852. A Mr Winter had advertised for a wife in the London papers, and his appeal came to the attention of a bunch of regulars at the Bull and Mouth Hotel. They thought the whole thing uproariously funny. Then one of them suggested having the Southerner on...

What they did began quite simply, but it was to develop into farce of a high order. They obtained a sheet of delicately perfumed paper and, laughing and joking over their mugs of ale, composed a *billet doux* claiming to be from a Miss Bailey. This was duly posted off to Mr Winter, who replied with great delight. A regular correspondence began, with the jokers at the Bull and Mouth dreaming up fresh sentiments to express each time, building up a word-picture of the fictitious Miss Bailey.

Eventually, Mr Winter could contain himself no longer and wrote passionately demanding a meeting with this lady of his dreams. The pranksters fair fell about the bar guffawing at their audacity, and after ordering another round of drinks launched into composing their master-piece. This was a long and detailed letter in which 'Miss Bailey' suggested that they meet at the hotel, when she would explain her position more fully and introduce Mr Winter to her relatives.

Next, the jokers chose one of their number who had a particularly smooth complexion and dressed him in a young lady's outfit, amid much mirth and merriment. 'She' retired to a private room hired for the occasion and awaited the arrival of Mr Winter. When he came, he was shown to the room, and the couple introduced themselves, the young man in drag playing his part with consummate tact. Then 'she' brought in her 'relatives' one by one; first, her loving brother, who bowed and shook hands with Mr Winter, keeping his face as stolidly expressionless as possible. Downstairs the partners in humour were doubled up with laughter, tears streaming down their faces. But one by one they recovered their composure enough to make the trip upstairs and put on a brief act of uncle, cousin, brother-in-law...

Finally, the imposters could stand it no longer and, to Mr Winter's amazement, flooded into the room and admitted it was all one big joke. Mr Winter took the whole jape in good part, had a hearty laugh, shook hands with everyone, including his potential 'fiancée' and proposed that he treat them all to wine and ale. Afterwards, he caught a train back to London, much sobered by his experience of Yorkshiremen.

CHAPTER 4

CRIME AND DRAMA

It is fair to say Yorkshire has had its villains. The following tales take us through the gamut of ruthlessness, madness and revenge, to the dangers of criminal over-confidence, courage against the evil-doers, fatal negligence and a question mark hanging over justice itself.

Robbers' Retribution

A certain false glory has attached itself to the highwaymen of old with which Yorkshire once abounded, preying on the hapless in out-of-the-way places and along lonely roads. This was long before an official police force existed or there were such things as telephones to summon help and radio cars to head off escaping highwaymen. In truth, the wrong'uns were no more than what we would nowadays term muggers, working individually or in pairs; and sometimes whole brigades of brigands would rampage over the countryside, terrorising the honest dwellers of the neighbourhood.

One such band was notorious in the East Riding; it was based on the eastern part of the Wolds, in the Driffield area. A formidable woman known as Peg Fyfe was queen of this robber band whose members never hesitated to carry out her most ferocious orders. Throughout the Riding, victims of her forays from a Wolds stronghold were only too glad to give what was demanded, for fear of even worse being asked.

In times when life was cheap and callous treatment was meted out by even the law-abiding folk to their own kind, when investigating such matters as witchcraft or 'persuading' defendants to plead in court cases, Peg excelled herself with one particular act which earned her the awesome title of 'Cruel Peg Fyfe'.

It happened like this. In Holderness, not far from Spurn Point, a small farmer eked a living from a few acres of land, helped by a labourer and a boy. Peg Fyfe had constantly demanded tribute from the poor farmer, who had so far managed to resist her demands, pleading poverty and hiding out of the way when her gang was seen approaching across the great bare flatlands.

But Peg thought of another cunning way to get what she wanted: the splendid great horses on which the farmer relied for his meagre living. And what better way than to get the farmer's boy to leave the doors open at night, so that her men would silently make off with them? Meeting the lad one day at work in the fields, she told him to do just this, threatening that if he so much as breathed a word to his master she would flay him alive.

The terrified boy returned to the farm that night, fear and duty struggling for mastery. Loyalty to his master won and he decided on a way to reveal the plot without actually telling his master. He went into the house and beckoned his master, putting his finger to his lips. Puzzled, the farmer followed the boy into the stables, where he again put his finger to his lips and indicated that the farmer should stand where he was. Then the boy went over to the horses and in a loud whisper recounted to them the story of the afternoon's episode in the far fields, and how sorry he would be to find them gone in the morning.

The farmer immediately understood what was going on and quietly tiptoed out of the stables. The boy retired to bed in the loft above the stables without exchanging another word with the farmer that evening but, of course, leaving the stable door open. About midnight he heard stealthy steps and he softly called out, 'Who's there?'

'Peg Fyfe!' came the reply.

With a flash and a bang a gun was discharged at them from the shadows and there was a cry of pain. Although the farmer instantly uncovered his lantern, no one was to be seen, so softly had the would-be thieves melted into the night. But in the morning there were bloodstains on the cobbles in the farmyard.

For a long time the lad lived in constant dread of Peg's threatened revenge. But the weeks, then the months, went by and nothing untoward occurred. In fact, the little farm, which was prospering quite well, went unscathed by the robber band. Bolder, the lad ventured farther afield from the house until one afternoon he went some considerable distance on an errand. To his horror the fearful form of Peg Fyfe arose from the reeds bordering the path. He looked wildly round for somewhere to flee but her grinning henchmen were on every side. She gave a signal and the lad was quickly stripped and bound.

The reader would feel faint if what happened then were described in detail here. Suffice it to say that Peg Fyfe carried out her terrible threat to the letter. The brave lad was determined to make no sound until the fiends began to strip the living skin from the palms of his hands and the soles of his feet. Then groans and screams spilled out. Satisfied with their evil work, the band melted into the scrubland, leaving the tortured youth to find his way back.

All night it took him to crawl and stumble home, the farmer and his family awake throughout it wondering what had become of him. When a faint knock came at the door, they rushed to open it, recoiling in horror at the dreadful sight that met their eyes. With a weak cry the lad fell to the rush-strewn floor, as gory a sight as ever the farmer could recall. He was tenderly wrapped in a blanket but died shortly afterwards.

Word of the outrage quickly spread among the communities in Holderness, and parties were soon out scouring the countryside. But no trace of the murderess was found. However, some years later, under different circumstances, Peg Fyfe was brought to justice and hanged. Tradition says she drew her last breath at a place called Gallows Hill between Market Weighton and Shipton. When one of her cronies was being taken to be hanged at York's Knavesmire, his wife called out from the crowd:

'Ah say, Tom, hev Ah ti set oor gardin wi taties this back end?'

'Ah deeant care what thoo diz,' called back Tom from the cart. 'Deeah what tha likes. Dammit all! Ah nivver was se' mad i' all mi life afooar!'

Dark Deeds Immortalised

Shakespeare is said to have penned the facts of a bloodstained Yorkshire drama under the title *The Yorkshire Tragedy* but is is not recorded in any of the standard collected works of the great bard. Scholars have pronounced it to have been powerful but crude and not at all in the manner of Shakespeare. The following is an account from another source of the dark deeds that are said to have been perpetrated at Calverley Hall in the early years of the 17th century...

The hall was the residence for 600 years of the family of that name. Walter Calverley, son and heir of William Calverley Esquire, married Philippa, daughter of Sir John Brooke, and had three sons, William, Walter and Henry. Walter Calverley was obsessed with dread that his three sons might be reduced to begging in the streets, such was the hard-up state they were in because of the family's dissipation and vices. He had decided that sooner or later he would have to save them from this dreadful fate by the simple expedient of murdering them.

This long pent-up state of intolerable apprehension came to a head when Walter learnt that his own brother had been committed to prison because of a security he had given on a debt which he was unable to discharge. This turned Walter's mind completely. Grabbing a dagger, he fell upon his eldest son, whom he spotted at play in the gallery at the hall, and stabbed him several times. He then carried the bleeding child to his mother's room. There the nurse was dressing another of the children. The clamour awoke the mother, who rushed over to the threatening figure of the father trying to get at the child whom the frantic nurse was sheltering. Philippa clutched the child in her own arms but, horror of horrors, the father killed the child while she held it. Then he turned his fury upon his wife, inflicting several wounds.

Walter, now crazed with bloodlust, dashed for his horse and rode into the neighbouring village, where the remaining child was at nurse. Meanwhile, a servant had been alerted at the hall and had ridden furiously into the village after Walter. The infant child owed its life to this circumstance and to the fact that its father was thrown from the horse as he galloped into the village. The servant was able to secure Walter and thereby averted further tragedy.

The father was brought before magistrates and freely admitted his crimes, explaining that he had harboured thoughts of doing away with the children for the previous two or three years. He also claimed that Philippa had kept dropping hints that he was not in fact the father of her children, and that she had several times put his own life in danger. It was a queer state of affairs and one which obviously left the magistrates in doubt about his real motives. He was committed for trial and, after being sent first to Wakefield since the Plague was raging at York, eventually ended up before the judges at York. Then Walter, who by any standards had proved a most unnatural sort of father, did a very noble thing. He refused to plead either guilty or not guilty, and was sentenced to be pressed to death. This was a very cruel and protracted way of persuading the defendant to plead, failure to do so resulting in a form of slow suffocation beneath ever-increasing weights. However, there was one inestimable benefit that the tortured victim had to keep before his fading eyes throughout the agonising hours - that if he did, in fact, hold his tongue, he would not forfeit his estates and property to the Crown if found guilty. And in his case it was a foregone conclusion that he would be.

Walter Calverley held out to the last despite the most terrible suffering and finally expired, executed in effect without even a proper trial. But his estate passed to his son Henry, and the estate remained in the family until 1754 when it was sold. Philippa, wife of the extraordinary murderer who in the end did the right thing for his family, recovered from her wounds and lived to a ripe old age.

Foul Murder Avenged

No one has ever explained why, back in the reign of Edward III, Sir John Elland of Elland also ran amok. He suddenly took it into his head to rally a body of friends and tenants and sally forth to the Manor Hall at Leeds, where they violently attacked and killed Hugh of Quarmby, Lockwood of Lockwood and Sir Robert Beaumont of Crossland. But do it he did, and in style, dragging Sir Robert from his wife and beheading him in the hall of his own house. Perhaps Sir John had a grievance to settle, or was avenging some murder committed and never recorded in the chronicles of the day.

Whatever the cause, the bloodbath frightened the wits out of the younger members of the victims' families, who fled across the border to Lancashire and took refuge with the Towneleys and the Breretons. When the eldest sons of the outraged families reached manhood they, in the tradition more usually associated with the vendettas of Sicily, crossed the Pennines bent on evening the score. The three young men from the Beaumont, Quarmby and Lockwood families lay in wait at Cromwell Bottom and, as Sir John Elland was returning to Rastrick, they ambushed and killed him.

Not satisfied with this, they then planned how to erase the name of Elland altogether. They hid in a mill near which Sir John's son, wife and child were due to pass on their way to church. As the family approached, the vengeance party rushed out of hiding and shot an arrow through the father's head, a mortal wound, and inflicted such grievous harm on the child that it died soon afterwards at Elland Hall.

The murder of the young knight and his infant son enraged the townsfolk of Elland, who took up arms and went in search of the killers. They soon caught up with the trio, and a desperate fight followed. Quarmby fell dead at the scene and the other two fled on their horses and by some luck outran their pursuers. The name of Elland was now extinct and the widow married one of the Saviles, the property passing into their hands.

Solomonic Settlement

On a less bloodthirsty note is the story behind a family fall-out at Malton, which was speedily settled with Solomonic wisdom. The site of Malton Castle, which had been demolished by Henry II, was chosen by Ralph, Lord Eure, to build his splendid mansion, which was completed at the end of the 16th century.

But his two grand-daughters fell out over ownership and the matter was referred for arbitration to Henry Marwood Esquire, of Busby Hall in Cleveland, who was then High Sheriff of the County of York. He wasted no time deciding the issue - he had the mansion pulled down and the materials divided between the two women, in 1674. He ordered, however, that the lodge and gateway be left standing 'as a monument to the folly and vindictiveness of family feuds'.

Dog-Lovers' Downfall

There can be few more bizarre tales in the annals of crime detection than that which came from the West Riding in the reign of King Charles I. Samuel Sunderland Esquire lived at Arthing Hall, near Bingley. He was a very wealthy man, having accumulated large quantities of gold coin, which he kept in bags ranged along two shelves in his house.

Two men from Collingham decided to have a go at Mr Sunderland's private hoard. They were cunning in the extreme and always ready to take extra pains to do the job right. They even bribed a blacksmith to fit their horses' shoes backwards so as to deceive pursuers. As they had done their homework thoroughly, they had no difficulty in entering Arthing Hall, stealing as much gold as they could lay hands on, and making a successful exit, although someone gave the alarm while they were still on the premises. They prudently left without offering violence.

They had unfortunately taken away more gold than their horses could carry, so had to dump some of it near Leeds, where it was found later. They arrived back at Collingham, congratulating themselves on their success. But they had made one slight mistake which was to prove their downfall. Being true Yorkshiremen they were dog-lovers and had taken one of their terriers with them on their nefarious expedition. Perhaps they had intended to foil any guard dog which might give the alarm, so that their dog could keep it company; or perhaps it was intended to warn them of anyone approaching. Whatever the reason for taking it with them, they somehow managed to leave it behind, tied to a chair leg in the very room from which they had so cleverly lifted the gold.

Meanwhile, back at Bingley, Mr Sunderland, his friends and neighbours, had gathered on the scene of the crime. Failing to make any sense out of the horseshoe tracks in the lane outside, they decided that the strange dog found inside the house must belong to one of the robbers. Therefore, it was reasoned that, 'if released', it would go straight home. Someone had the bright idea of hobbling its legs with a length of cord so that it would not run too fast for them to keep up, and they turned it loose. Sure enough, it limped its way directly to Collingham and stopped at the very house inside which the robbers were gloating over their haul piled up on the table in front of them. Needless to say, they paid dearly for their crime on the gallows at York.

Protecting His Property

The courage of Mr John Boyle in protecting his property at Ardsley more than 160 years ago illustrates the instinctive reaction of Yorkshiremen to trespassers bent on mischief. Without any doubt he would today have come off the worst in the eyes of the law, although at the time he was hailed as a public hero. Mr Boyle was a quiet-living gentleman getting on for 80. He had suffered a long illness which made him weak and frail. He lived with his wife and Elizabeth Bamforth, a servant girl, in a neighbourhood with a reputation for lawless behaviour. It became known that he had recently received his rents from some modest properties he owned and half-a-dozen ruffians decided they wanted their share, too.

Their forced entry into the house awoke the servant, who had the presence of mind to bolt a door which opened onto the landing from the bedrooms, and then woke up her master. The brave old man determined to tackle the intruders and armed himself with a carbine which he kept handy, although it had not been fired for two years. He slipped a pistol into his pocket and, followed by his wife who had equipped herself with a drawn sword, went bravely down the main staircase to tackle the robbers.

Taking the violent nature of the times and the absence of any means whereby the police - then existing only in a primitive form - could be alerted quickly, this was the only thing he could have done, apart from cowering in a locked room while his livelihood was stripped away from him. Mr Boyle spotted a man by the kitchen door and fired his carbine at him. Through the acrid fumes of the black powder discharge he saw him fall, badly wounded. The cowardly gang immediately took to their heels, leaving their stricken companion to crawl from the house with a trail of blood behind him.

When the authorities arrived, they caught and questioned the injured man - who turned out to be called Scott and to live nearby - but he had his own ideas of heroism and refused to divulge the names of his companions in crime. Two of the miscreants were, however, later caught. The death sentence on the three was commuted to transportation for life.

A 'Daft' Disaster

Yorkshire folk have always had a sweet tooth, and it was this fondness that led to a tragic loss of life at Bradford in the autumn of 1858.

This came about in an almost unbelievable way. A man named William Hardaker had been selling the popular lozenges on the market. He had bought them from a wholesale confectioner called Joseph Neal, in Stone Street. Mr Neal made the sweets himself, using quantities of gypsum mixed in with the sugar. For some odd reason this substance was known as 'daft'.

When he began to run short of his stock of 'daft' Mr Neal sent his lad out to the druggist's shop at Shipley for some more. It was all normal procedure, only on this occasion the druggist, Mr Hodgson, was off sick. The business was left in the hands of his assistant, a William Goddard, He did not know where to find the 'daft' so he went into the living quarters where his boss lay suffering from a feverish cold, and asked for further directions. Mr Goddard was told to go to a cask in one corner of the cellar.

Young Goddard somehow went to the wrong cask and instead of extracting 12 pounds of 'daft' took out 12 pounds of a similar-looking white substance - arsenic. Perhaps the lighting wasn't very good in the cellar, or there was no labelling system, but someone had certainly been remiss over the storage of dangerous chemicals.

Joseph Neal blithely mixed the 12 pounds of arsenic into 40 pounds of sugar, along with four pounds of gum, to be made into the lozenges. Of this lethal cocktail, William Hardaker acquired 40 pounds, of which he had by nightfall sold five pounds to the unsuspecting Bradford public.

It has been estimated that each lozenge contained nine and a half grains of arsenic, more than twice what is considered to be a poisonous dose. Since the lozenges weighed 16 to the ounce, it is reckoned that there was enough poison in circulation to kill nearly 2,000 people. Surprisingly, no more than 17 people died and 200 others were taken ill. Perhaps the consumers didn't like the taste or had some sense of foreboding.

Hodgson, Goddard and Neal were all charged with manslaughter; but the case against Goddard and Neal was withdrawn. The hapless Mr Hodgson, who should have kept better account of his stock, went through the ordeal of a trial at York before being acquitted.

A Question Of Justice

One of the traditional attributes of the Yorkshireman is a sense of fair play, enshrined in his great love of sport and of cricket in particular. But was Joseph Blackburn a rogue or the innocent victim of some mistake, and did the judicial system of 200 years ago give him a fair deal?

Born about 1770, he was well educated and articled to an attorney, after which he opened a practice in Leeds. He married well and had two children. He was well liked and respected in the profession. Twenty years on, however, his world fell about him over the faintest of shadows. A man who had formerly been his clerk brought an information against him - in other words, reported him - that he had been in the habit of removing stamps from old deeds and placing them on new ones, thus depriving the government of its slice of duty on these important legal transactions.

It was an extremely serious allegation but Joseph Blackburn was put on trial on a specimen charge, that of forging a £2 stamp on a mortgage deed of £180. After a lengthy prosecution case had been presented, the judge, Sir Simon le Blanc, seemed to think that the charge was clearly established and overruled every legal objection put forward by defending counsel. Joseph Blackburn was then called on to make his defence.

He made an impassioned speech to judge and jury affirming that he certainly was not guilty of the crime of which he stood accused. He had not heard the details of the indictment until he stood before the court and had no time in which to prepare an answer to it. He knew nothing of the particular deed referred to. If it had not had a proper stamp affixed to it the engrossing clerk must have surely seen it. In any case, when his house was searched by the authorities his account books had been taken away, so that he had been unable to trace the document in question.

He dealt at length with minute detail of how the stamping and checking was carried out, in an effort to persuade judge and jury that he could not possibly have done what was alleged, and concluded by saying that he hoped their decision would be the right one.

A host of witnesses then came forward to testify to his excellent character. But the judge summed up with some severity towards the prisoner and after an absence of only 15 minutes the jury returned with a verdict of 'Guilty'. As if that were not enough, a second charge was levelled at him concerning another deed. He was instantly acquitted. Blackburn was so affected by this decision that he had to be helped out of the court by his guards.

The following Wednesday he was brought into court to receive his sentence. Judge le Blanc tore into him... 'The thirst for money or the wish to grow rich by means more rapid than by patient industry has induced you not only to plunder the public revenue but to involve private individuals in distress, if not absolute ruin. By a series of ingenious contrivances you have been able, by imitating the stamp used in the conveyance of property, to injure the public revenue to a very considerable amount; and by affixing those forged stamps to conveyances and other instruments, you have put to hazard property in a very great extent.'

After the awful sentence - death by hanging - had been pronounced Blackburn appeared to be convulsed with such agony of mind that he had to be carried from the courtroom.

Three thousand people, mostly from Leeds, signed a petition which was sent to the Prince Regent. It was refused. A similar plea was made to the judge, who was as obdurate. Blackburn was duly executed at York and his remains buried at Rothwell.

Guilty or not guilty? How could such a matter be proved on such slender evidence? Why did we never hear evidence from the original complainant? Did the former clerk have a grievance? Did he commit the frauds himself, then divert attention to his former employer? Or was Blackburn, after all, a crook who used his highly respectable status to cover his fiddling?

CHAPTER 5

CHARACTERS IN PROFILE

There are many aspects to the make-up of the Yorkshireman. The
following examples portray patience (which must not be stretched!),
godliness, blunt speaking (tempered with wit), a capacity for making the
most out of a long life, and a touch of obstinacy.

The Bare-fisted Baronet

Sir Tatton Sykes, that grand old East Riding squire, is best remembered
for his researches into farm improvements. His keen eyes spotted that the
grass grew greener round his kennels on areas where bones had been
thrown for the dogs, and crunched up. But it is not generally realised what
a tough character he was and how he could keep up with the best of any
working men for stamina.

He would be up with the lark in summer and long before sunrise in
winter. After a frugal breakfast, perhaps with an apple tart and a drink of
fresh milk, he had been known to relieve a stonebreaker of his labours by
the roadside and send the man back to the manor house at Sledmere for
a snack. Meanwhile, Sir Tatton would apply himself diligently to the
gruelling task of breaking down the flinty chalk-stones which were then
used for road surfacing.

Sir Tatton was a splendid specimen of Yorkshireman, standing six feet
and weighing a muscular 11-stone maximum. He was renowned as a
boxer, with a punch not forgotten in a hurry. In those days men fought
bare-fisted. Clearly, his reputation was unknown to the two hulking louts
whom he encountered on one of his sheep-buying sorties into Pickering.
Thirsty after a morning driving hard bargains with farmers with whom he
enjoyed a mutual respect, he ordered a pitcher of ale at the bar of the inn
where he was staying.

The two drovers were standing near as the pretty barmaid placed the
refreshing drink down on the waxed oak bar-top. One winked at the other,
reached roughly past Sir Tatton and seized the ale. Sir Tatton watched as
the man drank it almost without stopping to draw breath and put the empty
container down with a smirk at his companion. Sir Tatton sighed gently,
a sigh such as no one else might have noticed, and quietly ordered another
drink. The drovers nudged each other gleefully. What an old fool this one
was! The barmaid set down the pitcher of ale and scarcely had Sir Tatton

moved his hand towards it than the other drover snatched it up in front of his very eyes and sank it with almost the same ease as his companion. He wiped the froth from round his mouth, and impudent merriment danced in his eyes.

Sir Tatton had a deceptively mild voice which he was very rarely known to raise. In the same quiet tone he ordered another drink and watched as the first ruffian grabbed it. Sir Tatton waited patiently until he had drunk the lot, then stood up. The two drovers grinned insolently. One belched loudly. Sir Tatton was a man of great patience; now it was sorely tried; he buttoned up his coat and told the first man to stand up. He did so, lurching slightly. Sir Tatton hit him, a straight left to the solar plexus. The man staggered, recovered his balance and tried to rush Sir Tatton, his arms flailing. Sir Tatton put up his guard, then shot a succession of piston-like jabs to the man's head and face. Blood spurted and the drover put his hands to his ruined mouth. Sir Tatton went in close, his iron-hard fists slamming into the man's belly. A swift uppercut caught the man on the chin and he slumped backwards against the wall, cracking his head and sliding down onto the floor.

It all happened so quickly that the other drover's reaction came too late to try to join in and help his mate. Now he got to his feet, an overweight, unshaven figure with bloodshot eyes and heavy jowls. He looked as if he could make mincemeat out of the trimly-built Sir Tatton. But within seconds he was given the same treatment as his fellow had got; it seemed as if the anonymous-looking 'gentleman' with the frank and open face had some kind of invisible shield around him through which the drover's bullying tactics could make no headway. Teeth - the drover's own - shattered and his lips split after two volleys of blows, then his paunch full of beer got a blistering salvo propelled by Sir Tatton's whipcord muscles. Before the man could recover his balance, he had one eye closed and his ears were singing with the resounding claps that Sir Tatton had playfully interposed on them between more punches.

Suddenly, the drover broke off combat. His pal was already crawling along the floor towards the half-open door - the other customers having fled the room and the barmaid standing in a corner, open-mouthed with amazement - and the drover jumped over him to be first out and away from this human windmill. Sir Tatton rubbed his knuckles, one of them slightly grazed where it had caught a button on one his victims' coats. He turned and smiled at the barmaid.

'Another pitcher of ale, please.'

Straight Off The Bakestone

If ever a man believed in striking while the iron was hot it was Samuel

Hick, of Micklefield. When he died in November 1829 in his 71st year, he had established a reputation not only as a first-class village blacksmith but as a popular Wesleyan preacher, who, like his brethren, travelled from place to place on a 'circuit'.

Samuel Hick was born at Aberford, one of 13 children. His family was so poor that it could not afford to give him a proper education, and by the time he reached manhood he could neither read nor write. He was 14 when he was bound apprentice to Edward Derby at Healaugh, near Tadcaster, to learn the blacksmith's trade. During his seven years' apprenticeship, he was often moved by strong religious feelings. He would follow one preacher, Richard Burdsall, for miles just to hear him preach; and, when he did, he would feel a sense of great blessing descend upon him.

Now it happened that, just before his time was served, Samuel was smitten by another great feeling - love. It would not be strictly fair to say that he began the wooing, rather that the girl took a strong fancy to him. He raised no objection when she came and sat on his knee one morning before the house was up and about. She was whispering sweet nothings in his ear when down came Mr Derby. He said not a word, but turned and went straight back up again to confer on the matter with his wife, still a-bed. He is credited with telling his wife that he believed their daughter 'was as fond of the lad as ever a cow is of its calf', but this momentary indulgence was swept aside by the anger of Mrs Derby, who insisted that the affair be brought to a swift end. The result was that young Samuel left that very day, depriving his lovelorn admirer of even the hope of a swift elopement.

Out in the big wide world on his own, Samuel did not waste time. He found a shop empty at Micklefield which his father took for him. Samuel set himself up in business and, after paying for his tools, found he had nothing left to eat or to buy food with. But he was strong and in excellent health - and he trusted in the Lord who, just as he had sent the ravens to feed his servant, somehow kept his energy levels up enough to do a day's hard work. His labours were rewarded when manna fell from heaven in a quite unexpected way. A man came into his workshop one day and told him that his wife had fed their pig until it was so fat that it was useless for the family. He offered to sell half of it very cheaply to Samuel Hick, who could only confess that, dearly as he would have liked to take advantage of this kind offer, he was totally without funds. The stranger said that he could trust Samuel and gave him his agreed share of the pig.

Samuel couldn't help telling a neighbour of his good fortune and could hardly believe it when the man offered to lend him £5, which he accepted. With this he paid the first man, and, after much hard work over his glowing fire and sparking anvil, he was able to repay the £5, besides selling off some of the excellent ham that he had salted away in his dry if cramped quarters at the shop.

Then Samuel Hick's thoughts turned again to love. This time it was not the romantic boy-meets-girl passion that had led to his dismissal as an apprentice, but the real thing: he needed a helpmate. The Lord once again came to the rescue, and chose Martha more for her endearing and practical character than for her good looks. It wasn't long before he said the right things to Martha, and they were united in holy matrimony at Spofforth church. As they left the church after the ceremony, a number of poor widows pressed round the couple, begging for alms. His heart was touched and without hesitation he emptied his pockets of all he possessed, saying to himself: 'I began the world without money and I will again begin it straight.'

Martha, who was five years his senior and had more realistic ideas about cash, said nothing, letting her new husband have his final fling. Then she took charge of the purse strings for the rest of their long and happy marriage. Samuel's business prospered ever after, and he never wanted for money again.

Not long after, he was converted through a vision that appeared to him in his sleep. His mother-in-law, who had been a member of the Wesleyan Connexion, had died, and she appeared to him dressed in white, took him by the hand and warned him 'to flee the wrath to come'. Samuel was ecstatic. 'My eyes were opened,' he declared. 'I saw all the sins I had committed through the whole course of my life. I was like the psalmist. I cried out like the gaoler. I said my prayers as I never did before.' He became a 'joined Methodist' and determined to become a preacher, committing himself to a code of Christian usefulness and strictly moral conduct. By 1797 he was active as a prayer-leader and exhorter in the neighbourhood of Kippax, Garforth, Barwick and Micklefield. Having the benefit of a horse, he could travel widely without difficulty. Within the next five years he became a local preacher on both the Selby and Pontefract circuits.

A tall, bony figure topping six feet, he had a quaint way of preaching, half-comic, half-solemn, so that one moment his listeners would be laughing, then in tears. He expressed himself in the broadest West Riding dialect. And when he wasn't travelling to deliver his impromptu sermons, he would treat his blacksmith's shop as a chapel, being renowned for the simple but striking homilies he delivered to rich and poor alike who called to see and hear him. It was through his efforts that a chapel was built at Aberford, his home town, and he chipped in with the first £20. Then he laid the first stone and preached the first words there.

It was said that his charity knew no bounds and that he would weep on hearing anyone's tale of distress. One day, going back home with a load of coals from the pit, he was stopped by a little girl who pleaded for just one piece of coal; her mother was ill and the family was without a fire.

Samuel Hick went with the girl to her home and found her story true. Then he brought his cart to the door and tipped the lot out, without even thinking of charging anything for it. On another occasion, a troop of soldiers, on a forced march, halted at Micklefield. Samuel's heart swelled with loyalty and sympathy. He quickly put before the men the entire contents of his pantry, buttery and cellar: bread, cheese, butter, meat, milk and beer. When Martha found out she ticked him off gently for not skimming the cream off the milk first. 'Bless thee, bairn,' he smiled, 'it will do them more good with it on.'

Samuel Hick was very fond of his pipe, but he gave even that up for a good cause. It happened like this. He once visited a poor aged widow and gave her sixpence, all he had in his pocket. She was so overcome with gratitude that he asked himself how many sixpences he must have spent on 'feeding this mouth of mine with tobacco'. He vowed never to take another pipe while he lived, promising to give to the poor what he saved from so doing. Soon afterwards, Samuel fell ill and his doctor advised him that this was an effect of breaking the tobacco habit so abruptly.

Samuel Hick was regarded as a bit of a weather prophet - not for any skill at forecasting it, but for summoning it as required. One day, during an excessive drought in Lincolnshire, he was seen to be restless and preoccupied. He explained that he was worried in case, after praying so hard for rain, it did not come. A brief shower is reported to have followed this intercession. Another time, he was about to hold a love-feast at Micklefield, from which folk as far away as Knottingley had been invited. But there was no flour in the house for the customary baking. He took two loads of corn to the local mill, where he was met with a blank stare, for the day was perfectly calm and the windmill was out of action.

'Never mind,' said Samuel, cheerfully, 'just put up your sails', which the miller did, and immediately a breeze sprang up and the machinery began turning. A neighbour, seeing the sails turning, also sent his own corn to be ground, but the wind quickly dropped.

When he retired from blacksmithing in 1826, Samuel had made enough money to travel more widely, even into Lancashire. His sermons were short, usually lasting half an hour. A friend urged him to use more method in his sermons, to which Samuel replied in typical fashion: 'I give it to them straight off the bakestone!'

Testing The 'Lowance

Accustomed as he is to blunt speaking, the Yorkshireman also has a quick wit. The two elements combined are well illustrated in this brief item from the farming scene of days gone by...

It was the custom in Victorian times for farmers to buy in quantities of ale for the use of his workers at the harvest. Naturally, this was not always of top quality. It would be allotted to the labourers at 'lowance time; for which it was taken out to the fields in large brown jugs covered with a clean cloth. Towards the appointed season, the farm foreman slipped into the brewing shed to get a foretaste of the ale set aside for his men (and women) labourers.

Through a half-open door, the farmer noted his foreman go into the brewing shed and followed him in.

'What's thoo up to, Zeek?' he inquired, politely.

Taken by surprise as he sipped from a ladle which he had tapped the barrel to fill, Ezekiel replied:

'Ah'm trying a sample o' this year's 'lowance ale.'

'And?' queried the farmer.

'Ah'm to thinking, if it were any worse we wouldn't be drinking it, an' if it were any better we wouldn't be getting it.'

The farmer was still trying to work that one out as Zeek walked past him, doffing his cap courteously; and the matter was never referred to again.

A Full Life To 169!

People who lived to a tremendous age have been few and far between in this country. Before the introduction of parish registers by Henry VIII in 1538 those few claimants to extreme longevity had no real proof to support their claims and we cannot be entirely sure that they were not decades out. The Countess of Desmond, for instance, was a married woman in Edward IV's time, and lived until the end of Queen Elizabeth I's reign, so you're talking about a lifespan of 140 years. She is said to have had a new set of teeth not long before she died, but it is not clear whether she grew them or had them fitted. She is also said to have died from a fever after breaking a leg while climbing a tree to gather nuts.

Another person who attained a great age was Old Parr, who died in 1635 aged 152, and who was buried among the eminent dead in Westminster Abbey. Nearer home, a Yorkshire farm labourer called William Hurst died at Micklefield in May 1853, allegedly aged 107. George Kirton Esquire of Osnop Hall, Bradford, was a remarkable foxhunter, following the hounds on horseback until he was 80 years of age; and when he died in 1796 he had reached 125. But none of these can rival the phenomenal age of one celebrated son of the North Riding - Henry Jenkins.

At the York Assizes of 1667 there were gasps of surprise when Henry Jenkins appeared as witness in a civil case and gave evidence that the tithes involved had been paid, to his knowledge, for 120 years or more. This remarkable man had appeared before the court the previous year to settle another claim, and had deposed that an ancient road had existed to a mill 120 years before! Henry Jenkins said he clearly remembered the great lamentations aroused by the dissolution of the monasteries.

Henry was born at Ellerton-on-Swale, near Catterick, and despite the lack of any official record of his birth Bishop Littleton told an antiquarian society in December 1766 that an entry had been found in an old household book of the Graham family at Norton Conyers which said that when he went to live at Bolton-on-Swale, Henry was already about 150 years old. Sir Richard Graham had written that he often questioned Henry in his sister's kitchen and found that his recollections agreed with known facts and chronicles.

When he was supposedly 162 years old, Henry Jenkins recalled that he had gone as a lad to Northallerton with a horseload of arrows for Flodden battlefield, which a bigger boy took on for delivery. Before the battle of Flodden, in Northumberland, in 1513, 500 soldiers were raised in the City and Ainsty of York to march against the Scots. The Scottish king, James IV, was killed in that encounter, and his body brought to York for exposure to public view. They were indeed stirring times that Henry Jenkins had lived through. Four or five people from the same parish of Bolton-on-Swale testified remembering Henry Jenkins as an old man ever since they knew him - and they themselves were centenarians.

After serving as butler to Lord Conyers at Hornby Castle, Henry retired in 1557 and earned his living by fishing in the Swale, which he also regularly swam when past the 100 mark. The local gentry thought him too old to work, so provided food and a small dole when he called at their houses.

Henry Jenkins died at Bolton-on-Swale, near Catterick, in December 1670, aged 169 years, and he had the distinction of having an epitaph composed for him by Dr Thomas Chapman, master of Magdalen College, Oxford, 73 years later. The classic ode, no longer discernible on the weathered tombstone, read:

Blush not, Marble
to rescue from oblivion the memory of
HENRY JENKINS,
A person obscure in birth
But of a life truly memorable;
For he was enriched With the goods of nature
If not of fortune;
And happy in the duration, if not the variety of his enjoyments;
And though the partial world despised and disregarded
His low and humble state
The equal eye of providence beheld and blessed it
With a patriarch's health and length of days;
To teach mistaken man
These blessings are entailed on temperance
A life of labour, and a mind at ease.

In those hard days you needed a constitution like an ox to survive at all into manhood. Henry Jenkins once said that his recipe for old age was drinking plenty of tar water and nettle soup, wearing flannel next to skin all the year round, a diet of plain bread and cheese, cold meat and onions washed down with cold water and a half-hour's walk before retiring to bed. One thing is certain: Henry always gave his age as approximate, which lends more credibility to his claim than if he had been more precise.

The Tailor's House

Some Yorkshiremen, having grown set in their ways, will dig their heels in obstinately over quite simple issues. But, as this story illustrates, they are also capable of learning from experience...

Seth was a tailor who had served three generations of folk in the remote Yorkshire Wolds village of Burythorpe. By dint of much economy, such as doing single-stitching when he ought really to have done double, and making do with bits from offcuts for less obvious details on suits, hoping the customer would not notice the weave did not quite match, he managed to amass a tidy sum. He and his wife and two daughters had lived long enough in the cottage on the top floor of which he had his workroom, and he had been thinking about taking on a couple of extra apprentices and turning the whole of the premises over to his trade.

He rarely bothered to talk things over with his wife, but she tactfully asked him one supper-time whether the time had not arrived for such a successful businessman as himself to consider building a proper house for the family. After only a moment's hesitation he came to the point.

'Nay, lass, I don't see us having a house built just yet. It'll cost too much and a half. Now there's a gamekeeper's cottage coming up vacant for rent at t'other end of t'village, seeing as Squire's sold up part o' t'estate.'

The tailor's wife shuddered. The cottage was a dismal hovel, full of damp, for she had been in one day to gossip with the gamekeeper's wife and had noticed the state of the place. It was overrun with mice and rats, since the gamekeeper's wife had an aversion to cats, which ruled out her keeping one to keep down the vermin.

Over the next few weeks Seth's wife kept on about the advantages of having their own home, such as never having to pay out rent again, but Seth was adamant that it would be good money down the drain. Not that he was a skinflint, but he had never been known to buy a sixpenny packet of needles when a twopenny one would do. However, when the village shopkeeper announced that he was about to retire, having made his pile, and have a house built for him with half an acre of good pastureland at the back, he changed his mind.

Seth swallowed his reluctance to part with any of his savings and went to see the local builder, who was only too glad to draw up plans for the new house for him. Part of the deal was that Seth would give him discount on a new suit he wanted running up, and though Seth was most unwilling to cut his costs for anyone, he reckoned that by agreeing he would surely get only the best materials from the builder. In any case, he mused, he could always find a way to take a short cut somewhere in making the suit that was not immediately evident to the casual eye; who bothered to check every inch of the lining throughout a three-piece?

The house - a quite substantial structure with proper foundations and its own water supply laid on by pipe from a nearby spring - began to rise, tier by tier of bricks. Seth became increasingly brooding at mealtimes and began gnawing at his fingernails, earning solicitous glances from his wife, who feared that perhaps he was having troubles in the workshop. One mild summer's evening he told her, 'I'm going down to see how t'new house is coming on,' and went out.

He found the builder supervising his workmen as they laid the beams across to support the first floor.

'I've been thinking,' began Seth, 'about t'house.'

'That's good on yer,' replied the builder, passing a claw hammer up to one of his men. 'And it's coming on well.'

'We could save a bit on it if we ran a course or two less bricks round the upper storey, couldn't we?' ventured Seth.

'Aye, and it'd make 't bedroom ceilings a bit low, wouldn't it?' observed the builder.

'True enough, but, then, we'll be spending most of our time upstairs lying down, won't we?' reasoned Seth.

The frown that crossed the builder's face decided Seth that something would have to be done about the fancy buttons ordered for the waistcoat. Would the builder really notice if they weren't quite as exclusive as he had stipulated? He could snip some passably showy ones from a secondhand waistcoat, of which he had a chest full.

The builder agreed reluctantly to lower the upper storey. But when Seth passed by a fortnight later another discussion ensued. Seth had noticed with consternation that the chimney was already going up.

'Hold on,' he told the builder. 'That chimney's quite tall enough. Leave it at that, and we'll save on the price of any more bricks, and your men's time.' Despite all the builder's pleas that it was absolutely necessary for the chimney to be of a certain height in order to function correctly, Seth heeded nothing. Forthwith the chimney pot was cemented on at that very level.

Shortly afterwards, Seth, his wife and their two unmarried daughters moved in. It was now late autumn and the nights drew in chilly. His wife lit the fire. Within minutes the room began to fill with smoke.

'Wind's getting up,' remarked Seth.

'Aye,' responded his wife.

Soon the whole ground floor of the house was full of stinging smoke, which billowed back from the fireplace. Seth retired to bed, cursing as he banged his head on the low rafters. Not long after, his wife crawled in beside him, having undressed and struggled into her night clothes while bending almost double.

'I had to dowse t'fire, smoke was terrible,' she told Seth. He groaned. The house would be really cold to get up to; he had always liked to leave a fire burning low, to keep in the heat for when he breakfasted at the crack of dawn.

After a week or two of hardship, and with the family by now suffering from continual hacking coughs, Seth sought out the builder. 'Now then,' he told him, 'it's about that house you built for me.'

'Yes,' said the builder, warily, thinking Seth had discovered some trifling economy he had made in its construction - but then, who bothered to measure the actual thickness of brick and plaster in their home, or check whether the wood in the roof trusses was properly seasoned?

'I've been thinking,' admitted Seth. 'Maybe you were right about the chimney after all. It does make the fire huff and puff a bit, now and then'.

The builder guessed that it did, for village gossip had come to his ears that the tailor's customers were finding his work less than satisfactory, what with his constant coughing and his increasing bad temper. Why, he had black rings under his eyes you could shoe plough-horses with.

'I think maybe we'd better have that chimney up to the height you mentioned,' said Seth, 'and while you've got t'ladders up, could you put an extra course or two of bricks on those upstairs walls?'

The builder got his notebook and pencil out and did some calculations. He quoted a figure equal to all that the house had originally cost, plus some. 'Surely there's some mistake,' he argued, 'after all, it's only t'same as letting a tuck out on a suit.'

The builder shook his head sadly, 'Not quite, you don't build houses with tucks in them. There's all the scaffolding to set up again, the small quantities of materials that I can't get on discount, the entire roof to dismantle, the problems of getting men to work on a short contract. Why, I could end up out of pocket on a job like this.'

Seth put his house up for sale, but there were no takers. Who wants to live in a home where the bedroom ceilings are so low you have to do contortions to get undressed, and where you can't light the fire very often because you nearly suffocate? Seth's wife was relieved when he went back to the builder and asked him to carry on with the work, throwing in a free made-to-measure suit as an incentive. While the work was going on, they couldn't return to their old cottage, as this was now entirely turned over to his tailoring uses. So they were forced to take a short tenancy on the old gamekeeper's cottage, which was such an unpleasant ordeal that in later years they shuddered to recall it.

When they were comfortably reinstated in their 'new' house, Seth softened a bit. Realising what his penny-pinching had almost cost him and his family, he began throwing in little extras free with his suits, which quickly earned him a reputation for fair dealing. He became a popular figure in the village, often dining out on the story of 'the house that was built twice'.

He and his wife lived happily ever after, cared for in their old age by their two spinster daughters.

CHAPTER 6

A CLUTCH OF ECCENTRICS

There is no shortage of eccentrics among Yorkshiremen, largely because they are independently-minded and like 'doing their own thing', which outsiders tend to misinterpret...

An Innocent In London

The Airedale poet, John Nicholson of Bradford, was a prime example of eccentricity. Son of a worsted manufacturer, he showed no inclination to follow in the family business, to which he was introduced on the ground floor, so to speak, as a wool sorter. He loved music and played the hautboy tolerably well. He often walked to Leeds, 16 miles away, to buy a reed for his favourite instrument.

His poetry first attracted public attention when he wrote a satire on a Bradford doctor in 1818. He next wrote a three-act drama entitled *The Robber Of The Alps,* which was performed at the Bradford theatre. This proved so popular that he sat down and penned *The Seige Of Bradford.* Encouraged by these modest successes and that of a book of poems inspired by his native Airedale, he quit his job as a woolcomber and began roaming the country in order to sell his printed work. During this period he published *Lyre Of Ebor* and would have gone on to greater heights had not he been too fond of the bottle. His spendthrift habits soon got him into difficulties and his wife and family would have suffered greatly had not George Lane Fox, Esquire, of Bramham, twice elected M.P. for Beverley, befriended him and bailed him out from time to time. It was an astonishing relationship between a landed gentleman and a young man to all intents and purposes a bit of a ne'er-do-well.

In October 1827 Mr Lane Fox generously gave him £20 with which to straighten out his affairs for once and for all. John Nicholson promptly gave £4 of this to his wife and with the rest set off for London with a load of his printed works. The innocent from the provinces did not know the ways of the big city, and he thought he was onto a good thing when he fell in with a group who included a barrister and sundry young gentlemen. They

44

thought it great fun to invite this character from up North to the Drury Lane theatre, paying for his ticket. His quaint behaviour, his odd dress - blue coat, corduroy breeches and grey yarn stockings - attracted the attentions of a number of city swells, determined to have a good laugh at his expense. When they asked him where he got his stockings from, he answered truthfully that he had knitted them himself on one of his strolls across to Leeds to buy a reed for his beloved wind instrument. The Londoners fell about laughing at such a preposterous idea. It was, by the way, quite common for Yorkshire folk of both sexes to knit useful articles to make the most of time spent sitting or walking.

'Nay, lads, steady on,' protested the gentle poet, when their ragging got a bit out of hand. Soon the bit of fun degenerated into a squabble, then a scuffle, and before long poor John, overwhelmed and confused by the goings-on, knocked someone's pigtail askew. The poor fellow was hauled off to the local watch-house. Next day he was brought before the magistrate, who joined in the general merriment and discharged the prisoner. The daily papers made a riot of the incident, which they headed, 'The Yorkshire Poet in trouble'.

Although he returned home with only a halfpenny to his name, John Nicholson's faith in London as the great market for his works remained unshaken. After a few months he again visited the metropolis, this time with his wife in tow. Meanwhile, his publisher went bankrupt and his large stock of books, including those of John Nicholson, was auctioned. Unfortunately, he had paid for the paper, and the books went for less than half-price.

Much chastened by this calamity, he returned to the hard labour of the woolcombing bench to earn his living. Nevertheless, he took great pleasure in composing his poems, which included such immortal titles as A *Description Of The Low Moor Ironworks* and *A Walk From Knaresborough To Harrogate*. He came to a tragic end, after falling into the Aire near Shipley, while negotiating some stepping stones at night. He had dragged himself out of the chill waters, but collapsed exhausted on the bank, and perished of exposure before anyone passed by.

African Adventure

Given enough space, we could go on at length on Yorkshire explorers, who needed to be a bit eccentric to do what they did. Take, for instance, Colonel James Harrison of Brandesburton Hall, who at the turn of the century brought six pigmies back from his adventures in Africa. They were exhibited in London, some dying and the others being returned to their native habitat, then popularly referred to as 'Darkest Africa'.

Another explorer was Squire Waterton, of Wakefield, whose travels in the tropics involved wrestling with a crocodile and other bizarre adventures.

We should also mention Christopher Pivott, who died in 1802 aged 93 years. A former soldier, he was a carver and gilder of York, where soon after settling he had his house burnt down. Whereupon he made the oddest of resolutions: that he would never henceforth lie down in a bed. This undertaking he kept throughout the last 38 years of his life. He slept on the floor, in a chair, with his clothes on; but never again in a proper bed.

Another Yorkshireman stuck by a point of principle to the degree of eccentricity. He was John Dufreni, for many years a merchant in Leeds, who had refused to answer questions at his bankruptcy hearing. He was sent to prison - and there he stayed for the next 43 years, dying behind bars in 1856 at the age of 83.

In Fear of The Law

Old John lived near Well, a lovely spot with fine views of the purple-stained Hambleton Hills clear across the Vale of York. He farmed in a small way, though he belonged to a family of sheep doctors. These were a sort of unofficial vet who would in an emergency also set a broken arm or treat a sprained ankle among the farm labourers on whose intensive efforts the great estates depended in the years just before the Great War. Two of his cousins had left the land to join the police force, being of substantial height and physique, and of a certain level of education.

However, John had neither the stature nor, perhaps, the brightness of intellect necessary to become a constable. But he did have a healthy regard for the law, which at times manifested itself as a phobia. To illustrate this, let me recount how one day he was walking one of the huge fields that had just been ploughed, checking on the soil condition, when he heard a strange sound. Plodding along the furrows to the end of the field where it curved to follow a lane sunk into the slope, he beheld a very scruffy-looking tramp hollering some strange ditty at the top of his voice.

John, who had been brought up in the good old Wesleyan tradition, winced at the fellow's discordant efforts to sing; he himself was a staunch member of the chapel choir and could not imagine why any self-respecting person should want to make such an exhibition of himself in public. Having called out to the man to shut up and go home, and meeting with no response, John picked up a clod of earth and lobbed it gently towards the source of the noise. It spattered on the ground a yard away from the tramp, who immediately fell silent. Then the man stared up at John, silhouetted against the skyline, and pointed an accusing finger at him.

'Right, you there! I'll 'ave the law on you, I will.'

Seeing John blanch, he pursued the advantage, shaking his fist.

'I'm going to fetch a policeman right now!' he blustered.

John turned and fled as fast as he could across the lumpy soil, stumbling in panic, and twice falling full-length in the furrows. When he reached his little cottage, he ran upstairs and, without taking off his muddy boots or jacket, dived into bed, pulling the sheets over his head. And there he cowered until his wife came in from her duties at the big house where she was in part-time service. She found him gibbering with fear and quite unable to account for his strange predicament.

It took John a day or two to recover from the shock, and it never occurred to him that the tramp had had a good laugh at his expense.

Some put his odd phobia down to a threat he was supposed to have received from a policeman as a boy, that if he misbehaved he would be straightaway taken off to the public hangman. Whatever it was, it made a lasting impression on him.

Marksman On Ship

Incidentally, a cousin of John's from a neighbouring village, called Myers, went to sea as a youth. While on a round-the-world voyage in a fast sailing ship carrying goods from one country to another, his expertise as a marksman was called upon. It happened that one day the Chinese cook on board ran amok, chasing the sailors round the deck with a wicked-looking kitchen knife. Finally, the first mate, a fearless and well-built Geordie, confronted the cook, armed only with a marlin spike, and launched such a ferocious counter-attack on him that the raving oriental retreated and climbed up the rigging to the forward crow's nest, where he established himself in a position from which he could not be dislodged without grave risk to anyone attempting to do so.

Although the Chinaman was no longer a threat to the crew, it was a bit of nuisance having him aloft, so the captain of the vessel called on Myers to take a pot-shot at him, knowing that one of the reasons for his joining the ship originally was that his marksmanship was a bit too keen; the local landowner had felt his poaching activities had gone on for long enough, and had taken steps to bring the law into the matter (it is not recorded how his cousin John viewed this!). Deciding discretion was the better part of valour, Myers had hastily left the area and gone to Liverpool, where he joined the four-master's crew. With him had gone his trusty rook-rifle with which he had brought down so many pheasants and rabbits. Now the captain sent for him and his rifle.

'Bring that man down!' he ordered.

Myers raised the barrel of his gun, sighted, paused, then gently squeezed the trigger. High above their heads, the Chinaman jerked like a puppet on a string, clutching his bruised hand. With a clatter, the knife came tumbling down to the deck. A sailor who picked it up remarked that its razor-sharp blade was badly scored near where it joined the haft.

'Good shooting, Myers,' said the captain, 'But I said to bring the man down.'

Myers felt it better to say that he had missed than admit that he had baulked at aiming deliberately to kill a fellow human being.

Not Quite So Dim

To be dimwitted did not necessarily mean that one had lost such mental powers as to be at a disadvantage in early Victorian times, when a certain low cunning was often necessary in order to survive. Tom Moman was generally regarded as a half-wit in the northern part of the East Riding. He spent part of his time in the workhouse, and when not there did odd jobs such as cattle driving and running errands. Many tales were told of his tricks, for despite his label he was quite a shrewd character in his own way.

This story illustrates his nature well. In a hamlet near Bridlington lived a mean and miserly man who delighted in driving a hard bargain. He farmed a small plot, one part of which he had set with potatoes, the harvest from which he had made into a large 'clamp' at the top end of his field. One dark night Tom Moman knocked at the door with a large and heavy sack of potatoes for sale. The smallholder, knowing he was dealing with one of weak intellect, bartered him down a to price of sixpence. As he left, Tom was invited to bring some more, at the same price. After a moment's hesitation he agreed and the miser closed the door on him, then rubbed his hands with glee.

Tom brought sack after sack, every few nights, and was duly paid for them at the same miserable price. The smallholder gloated over his ill-gotten gains. Then he thought of a clever idea: he should offer Tom a little work - to be paid for at a pittance, of course. He asked him to empty the potato pie and wheel all the contents into an outhouse. Tom nodded dumbly and went out. He never came back. When the man went outside he discovered why: his potato clamp was almost gone. It had been rifled by Tom in revenge for being over-reached on the original sale of potatoes, which genuinely were Tom's to sell. The mean old man had been buying his own potatoes from him!

Tom, incidentally, died miserably, frozen in a snowdrift near Thirkleby in 1823.

A Professional Mourner

The nickname 'Fond' originally meant daft or feeble-minded, and no doubt we get our description of someone being 'fond' of his girl as meaning that he is out of his mind with love.

At one time, no funeral was complete in Beverley without the attendance of Fond Kit. He could almost be described as a professional mourner, though he turned up punctually at a variety of other events, such as the arrival of the mail coach, smartly dressed, with clean shoes, blue stockings, knee breeches and soft cap, looking folk direct in the face, his face wearing a meaningless smile and with his left hand open and extended and the wrist clasped in his right hand. He would repeat his parrot cry: 'He' ya a hawp'ny?'

The bestowal of such a modest gift by bemused mourners or travellers would fill his simple heart with childish pleasure and he would bow and scrape with gratitude. Fond Kit was not short of money; he would take the money to his sister Sally, with whom he lived. A halfpenny was all he desired and to promote its offer he would repeat from memory the entire tenth chapter of 'Ninnymiah' (Nehemiah) or tell a tale about 'a man wiv a heead as soft as a boiled tonnip, an what ran ageean a wall and smashed it.'

Simple-minded as he might have seemed, Fond Kit had not always been so. He was once a bright, keen boy who worked for his father and mother at the Fleece Inn, Beckside, Beverley. A party of noisy soldiers was billeted on them and the lad was kept busy running up and down the steep steps into the cellar bringing up frothing jugs of beer for their inexhaustible thirst. One day one of the soldiers decided to play a practical joke on Kit. He got a white sheet, slipped into the cellar while Kit was engaged elsewhere, and draped it over himself. When Kit next came down, the 'apparition' gave three sharp knocks on a barrel and rose eerily from behind a cask.

The boy dropped his jug and fled screaming up the stairs. The shock unhinged his mind, and from that day he became incapable of doing any useful work and relied on his family for support. His experience explained why if anyone offered him a shilling he would run away, for a shilling to him represented the King's money, the emblem of enlistment; and that meant soldiers.

CHAPTER 7

INTO THE UNKNOWN

Yorkshire has never been short of clever folk willing to exploit the fear of the unknown, often in quite harmless ways. But there have been many claims of genuine 'second sight'.

The Grip Of Superstition

It is hard to imagine the grip that superstition had on ignorant people's minds even into the later years of the last century. By ignorant people we mean a large proportion of the population: people who in many cases never travelled beyond the boundaries of their own parish, who could not read or write, who knew nothing of how their own bodies or natural phenomena worked, or of the dangers of infection. Any mishap or illness was put down to the work of evil spirits, and, if you could lay the blame at the door of some old crone who spent her days friendless in a decrepit cottage, so much the better. Once someone was named as a possible witch, the suggestible populace of an area would suffer a sort of mass hysteria and engage in a 'witch-hunt', with often frightful consequences.

Some cleverer people exploited this constant dread among the vast uneducated, and professed to be able to bring about a change in the fortunes of other people - for a fee - as well as to counteract the 'spells' which folk honestly believed had been cast upon them. One of these was Bartholomew Preston, known as the Charmer of Swine. The name had nothing to do with any magical power over farm animals, but to the East Riding hamlet near Hull, where he lived.

This notorious wizard was born in the latter years of the reign of the first Elizabeth. His sister Margery was a local bonesetter and midwife. Even her skill gave rise to suspicions that she dealt with the spirit world; such was the risk one took merely by having an intuitive, if unscientific, grasp of basic medical principles. After her death the finger of suspicion pointed at Bartholomew, who foolishly encouraged the belief in his 'powers'. He stated that he had dealings with the fairies. People who had had things stolen from them came to him for advice and, if he was not able to tell them exactly what had become of them, he gave them some clue. If anyone came and told him that their cattle had been bewitched he could usually tell them what colour the beast was.

He was a quack who professed a knowledge of magic to help out his natural talent for healing, and folk came from far and wide to consult him. However, tongues wagged and his publicly professed acquaintance with the powers of the unseen made enemies. A number of former 'patients' were willing to reveal that he had worked this or that piece of magic. It was recalled that he had been called to attend a sick child at Hull and had brought about its death by witchcraft. But when a constable came to Swine with a warrant from his arrest, Bartholomew Preston made up the matter with the child's aggrieved father.

Things came to a head when Preston was sent for to attend a young man at Paull who was 'strangely visited'. Preston simply tied a handkerchief round the young man's neck and assured his friends of his recovery. There the matter might have ended had not the sick man cried out after Preston had gone that 'the rats which was on the handkerchief was like to kill him'. Then he died. A boatman named Wintringham affirmed the truth of this, and it was reported to the magistrates. But whether a case was ever brought is not known, for Bartholomew Preston, the Charmer of Swine, discreetly faded out of public notice, possibly sensing the nearness of the pillory, the water ordeal and the crackling faggots.

Horse Frozen Still

Old Nanny Rowley, of Weaverthorpe on the Yorkshire Wolds, was much feared as a witch. It was said that a man against whom she had a grudge passed her cottage driving a horse with a heavy load; when opposite her door, it stood frozen still and refused to budge until he rushed into the house and struck her in the face, causing her to bleed and thus put an end to her power. Then the horse proceeded without difficulty. And Nanny Thrusk, who lived at Bonwick, a village near Skipsea no longer on the map, is said to have caught some mischievous lads driving away her donkey and transfixed them with the power of her eye so that they could not move a muscle until she released them from her power.

Unforeseen Disaster

There used to be no shortage of fortune-tellers up and down the Ridings. Usually they provided pleasure and amusement, gratifying their clients by telling them what they already secretly knew or hoped for. Among these was Rebecca Hird of Bridlington, who would tell fortunes, mainly to women who did not wish to die as old maids.

John Hepworth of Bradford also had a reputation as a fortune-teller; but even his skills could not predict for him the drastic consequences of one of his rituals. He had been called out to Blackshaw, near Halifax, by Robert Sutcliff, a poor weaver whose neighbours were accustomed to playing all sorts of pranks on him, to the degree almost of persecuting the old man. Sutcliff was convinced that his house was haunted by evil spirits; and who better to rid the place of them than the celebrated John Hepworth?

Sutcliff's eyes opened wide as, with great solemnity and muttering incantations, Hepworth poured human blood mixed with hairs into a large iron bottle as part of his spell to exorcise the cottage where the weaver lived. Then Hepworth corked the iron container tightly up and placed it on the fire, telling Sutcliff to leave it undisturbed for a while. Entranced by the whole procedure, Sutcliff sat hunched up close to the fire listening to the fizzings coming from within the iron bottle.

The fortune-teller left for home but had gone only to the end of the road when he heard a tremendous bang. Part of the cottage wall flew out into the road, the roof caved in and smoke and glowing cinders billowed everywhere. The pressures generated inside the magic capsule had proved too much for even the iron, and the thing had gone off like a bomb, killing the unfortunate weaver.

The Judge's Charm

Lord Chief Justice Holt once had an Otley woman brought before him accused of witchcraft. She denied the charge vehemently but said she had a wonderful ball which never failed to cure the ague. The charm was handed to the judge, who recognised it as one he had made himself many years before, to get himself and his companions out of a difficult position. When as law students they ran up a rather large bill at an inn and were unable to pay, Mr Holt noticed that the landlord's daughter looked very ill and, posing as a medical scholar, asked what ailed her. Told that she suffered from ague, the 'doctor' made a great performance out of gathering various herbs, mixed them with great ceremony, rolled them up in a piece of parchment, scrawled some weird characters on it and, to the amusement of his companions - who nearly gave the game away - he tied it round the young woman's neck.

To his amazement, an immediate cure followed. When the 'doctor' offered to settle the outstanding bill the grateful landlord refused it and the party were only too glad to leave the inn and go home.

Now the charm had come into his hands again - and before him stood a woman accused of conjuring with evil spirits but who had most likely played on the same shadowy aspects of human nature that enabled the young law student to 'faith heal' a sick girl. Sadly, the outcome of the case is not recorded but it is to be hoped that the judge's secret knowledge - which he could hardly reveal to the world - helped him towards compassion and mercy, and that he at least saved the woman from the terrible punishments that society ordained for anyone treading in such realms.

A Royal Haunting

You don't have to go far in Yorkshire without encountering a ghost story. There are few localities without one, and 'ghost walks' are an established feature of the York scene, the participants being assured they will hear the echoes of Roman legions tramping as they descend to the former street level. With a bit of imagination they might, too. All good, clean fun, and just what the tourist expects. So much has been written about ghosts in the county that I don't propose to devote much space to the subject in this present book. But I will give an account of just one haunting, and that so brief as to have been, perhaps, an illusion brought on by flickering candles and ancient oil-paintings... or was it?

Nappa Hall is a picturesque dwelling dating from the 15th century with a large battlemented tower at one end, and a smaller one at the angle where a shallow wing projects from the face of the building. It stands in a remote area of Wensleydale, not far from Askrigg. Behind the hall a green hill covered with flowers rises steeply; the scar beyond is said to have given its name to the house, Nappa signifying 'wild flowers'. Its pearly grey stones face a wall three or four feet thick in parts, and its rather churchlike shape belies the fact that it is a rare example of a fortified farmhouse, built originally to withstand the raids by the Scots.

For centuries it was the ancestral home of the Metcalfes, who from time immemorial held high office in the county. The tower, the great hall and the minstrels' gallery are now blocked off for safety reasons. Up to the middle of the last century there were three floors in the tower, with a newel staircase leading to them; but the solid black oak joists were removed. There was a kitchen, too. Every bit of the oak panelling was taken away and the ancient furniture, which for generations formed a part of the old house, was also removed. Among these spoils was a carved bedstead, slept in by Mary Queen of Scots when, during her imprisonment at nearby Castle Bolton, she was allowed to spend two nights at Nappa as the guest of Sir Christopher Metcalfe. She left behind a pair of hawking gloves, which passed into the possession of a Mr Barwick, of Low Hall, near Leeds. Now the remaining rooms and the adjoining living quarters are in private hands, and the occasional guests there are offshoots of the Metcalfe family, who have their own one-name society, and who are made especially welcome.

More than 100 years ago, a couple who were travelling through that wild and rugged scenery stopped off to view this lonely place. In their diary they wrote that the spirit of Queen Mary was said to visit Nappa. They recorded an account by a young woman who had stayed there only a few years previously, in 1878:

'I was in the hall, playing hide and seek with the farmer's little girl, a child about four years old. The hall was dimly lighted by a fire and the light from a candle in a room in the east tower. While we were at play someone entered the hall from the lower end and walked towards the dais. Thinking it was the farmer's wife, I ran after her and was going to touch her when she turned round and I saw her face; it was very lovely. Her dress seemed to be made of black velvet. After looking at me for a moment she went on and disappeared through the door leading to the winding stone staircase in the angle turret of the west tower. Her face, figure and general appearance reminded me of portraits of Mary Queen of Scots.'

At the time of the vision the bedstead slept in by the ill-fated Queen was still at Nappa. There was also a reputedly haunted bedchamber at the eastern end of the house, said the travellers: 'We went up there and certainly the room has not a cheering aspect. The walls are panelled and painted a dull green; one or two of these panels open and reveal closets within them. The wife of the farmer who now tenants Nappa laughed, however, as she showed them, and said she never saw any ghosts.'

I myself have stayed at Nappa in recent years and, if there was any spot in Yorkshire where I would expect to see or sense a ghost, this was it. But, although the house feels steeped in age and history, it certainly is not spooky!

Well now, you've sampled the Yorkshireman in many of his moods, and seen most of his virtues and vices at work. It will do for a start. I hope in a subsequent book to give you an idea of the weather he endured in olden days, of some of the natural wonders that have dumbfounded him; the hazards of his callings, the challenges he met and feats he accomplished; and enlarge on how he spent what spare time his labours allowed.

Alex Marwood.
Driffield, February 29 1992.